The ring of the telephone shattered the stillness of the night. Bill Ranger sat up abruptly in bed, and took a moment to get his bearings. It wasn't that late, just about 11:30, but he had turned in unusually early—especially for a Saturday night.

It wasn't Bill's habit to answer the phone, so as usual he let the machine pick up. Too many times the caller turned out to be an old girlfriend making one last attempt at reining in the confirmed bachelor. The fifty-two-year-old Navy reservist sat in the dark and listened for a while, not really wanting to get out of bed and still hazy from the deep sleep that had enveloped him. But the familiar baritone at the other end of the line startled him into full alertness, especially when he heard the words, "I want to be buried at Arlington Cemetery."

Throwing off the covers, he sprang out of bed and picked up the receiver. By the time he crossed the room, the machine had recorded a solid minute of the frantic diatribe.

"Akers!" Ranger barked into the phone. "What are you talking about?"

"I shot Nancy . . ."

ST. MARTIN'S PAPERBACKS TRUE CRIME LIBRARY TITLES BY LISA PULITZER

A Woman Scorned

Fatal Romance

FATAL
Romance

A TRUE STORY OF OBSESSION AND MURDER

LISA PULITZER

St. Martin's Paperbacks

FATAL ROMANCE

Copyright © 2001 by Lisa Pulitzer.

Cover photograph of Nancy Richards Akers © Tom Wolff; photograph of rose by Laura Wyss.

ISBN: 0-312-97580-5

Printed in the United States of America

St. Martin's Paperbacks edition / July 2001

10 9 8 7 6 5 4 3 2 1

To four of the most important people I know: To the prolific Joan Swirsky, who first introduced me to publishing with our collaboration on *Crossing the Line*, for her tireless effort and brilliant insights. To Cynthia Blair, queen of prose, for the hours she devoted and the expertise she provided. To Amy Beth Wapner, editor and friend, for putting me back on the right track, and keeping me focused. And to Douglas Love, my faithful editor and loving husband, for his selflessness and support. Although their names do not appear on the cover, let it be known that these four special people were instrumental in the writing of this book.

ACKNOWLEDGMENTS

First, I would like to extend my sympathies to the family and friends of Nancy Linda Richards Akers and Jeremy Ray Akers, whose lives have been irrevocably changed by this terrible tragedy.

To Finny, Zeb, and Isabelle, the real victims, who lost their beloved parents, my sincerest hope that they may go on to heal, and continue to hold dear all of the special qualities that made their parents cherished by their friends and family.

To all of the friends, family, and associates of Nancy and Jeremy Akers, who graciously agreed to speak with me about the couple, I extend my heartfelt thanks.

Gratitude to Finny Akers, Emily Karoyli, Kinley Mac-Gregor, Marvin Moser, Adam Lenkin, Avery Drake, and the others who chose to remain anonymous.

Having covered the crime beat for nearly ten years, I have learned that there are no persons more helpful to a journalist than the police officers who work the beat. Once again, that has turned out to be true.

My gratitude to Sgt. Joseph Gentile and Officer Anthony O'Leary of the Public Information Office of the DC Metro Police Department who went out of their way to accommodate my request for information.

To Sergeant Michael Farish of the Second District, who acted as lead detective and supervisor on the Akers case, I extend my deep appreciation for his time, honesty, and integrity.

Gratitude to US Park Police Officer Vincent Guadioso, who made himself available to be interviewed, and who was forthcoming in his information and recollections. And to Sergeant Robert Mclean of the Office of Public Information.

To Gunny Sergeant Phil Mehringer, Operations Chief, Division of Public Affairs, of the Headquarters of the US Marine Corps, and Lt. David Nevins, thank you for your help and expediency in providing me with the service record and information pertaining to Captain Jeremy Ray Akers.

Appreciation and gratitude to Elizabeth Burt of the Sheffield Public Library, and Judith Reinfeld and Flo Sinsheimer of the Scarsdale Public Library.

To Alan Soschin, I extend my sincere thanks for your time and insights.

To Dennis "Dawg" Thun and Tom Downes, who selflessly served our great country in the United States Marine Corps, and graciously shared their experiences with me, I am grateful and proud.

A heartfelt thanks to Nancy's fellow romance writers, Mary Kilchenstein, Kathleen Gilles Seidel, Katherine Karr and Ann Marie Winston, all of whom agreed to speak with me to help to educate Nancy's three children about how very special their mom really was.

I extend a special thank you to Jeremy's longtime friends, Don Boswell, his law school roommate, Bill Ranger, a devoted friend, and Raymond Walker, his childhood pal.

To Nancy A. Lemke, the mother of James Lemke, thank you for sharing your time and impressions with me.

On the Web, I would like to extend my gratitude to Barbara Deane, Gwen Richardson and Jaymie Frederick, Deanna Shlee Hopkins, Bill Crumlett, Arthur Davis, Mike Lerp, Bill Ervin, and members of the Thundering Third.

Gratitude to Tom Fickling, James Baird, and Glen Randall of the Sigma Chi fraternity and Debbie Purifoy and Lynn Frunzi McColl of the University of Alabama. And to Jim Grant, director of communications at the Kent School, for his help, and the lovely lunch I was treated to while visiting.

My gratitude to J.P. Cobleigh, Barbara Young and Monica Monterroso.

And a special thanks to Charlie Spicer, Dorsey Mills, John Rounds and Richard Onley of St. Martin's Paperbacks for their enthusiasm, support and patience, and to my agent, the great Madeleine Morel.

"Remember that in a romance, because you are talking about people, and the conflict between people, between characters, that as you resolve the conflict, you are also going to be talking about changes in the characters, how the people will be different at the end of the story than they are at the beginning of the story."

—Nancy Richards Akers speaking
to a group of writers at a workshop
in Harpers Ferry, West Virginia, in 1997

CHAPTER ONE

DRESSED NATTILY IN A SPORT COAT AND TIE, ADAM LENkin walked at an easy pace along the glass-enclosed breezeway of The Kennedy Center's Hall of Nations, his thick fingers embracing the delicate hand of his girlfriend, Athena.

Flags of every country stood at attention as the couple strode the music hall's plush red carpet, and stepped out onto the River Terrace to take in the breathtaking views of the Potomac River.

The intoxicating scent of the mild night air was a magical blend, Adam thought, of Athena's heady perfume and the fresh spray of water from the river that lapped gently below them. The summer season was still several weeks away, and earlier the thermometer had climbed to a balmy 85 degrees. But by nightfall it had dropped nearly twenty points, and the thin layer of haze that had lingered over the Capital City for much of the day had proliferated to a dense umbrella of low-lying clouds, obscuring much of the balcony's panoramic vista.

It was nice to have Athena in town for the weekend, Adam thought as he pulled her close, gazing over her shoulder at the shimmering white lights of the Memorial Bridge in the distance. Her job as a stewardess for American Airlines kept her traveling between her home in Dallas, Texas, and all points across the United States, but her busy flight schedule often conflicted with his own business trips. As a sports agent for several of the Professional Golf Association's most talented players, Adam was constantly traveling to tournaments in Florida, Texas, and California where he brokered profitable endorsement deals for the golfers he represented.

Descending the stairs to the Plaza Lobby of the sprawling arts and entertainment center, Adam turned his attention to the crowd of people milling about. A gentle wind blew off the river as he and Athena exited the spectacular concert hall and headed for the busy parking area. As they walked the cement pathway, chatting about the musical performance they had just enjoyed, they were treated to one final number by the Sonny Sumpter Quartet, who were wrapping up their free outdoor concert.

Gallantly, Adam opened the door of his polished Toyota 4-Runner for Athena and helped her into the passenger seat. A faint breeze tousled strands of his thinning hair as he rounded the sport utility and hopped in next to her. Glancing in his rearview mirror, he took one last look at the sprawling white cement structure until it faded into the black of night. Merging onto the Rock Creek Parkway, the couple headed for Adam's home, a route that had become so familiar to him during the past five years that his car almost drove itself.

After a short ride, Adam exited the narrow two-lane roadway that winds sinuously along the Potomac, listening attentively as Athena chatted with enthusiasm about the evening's musical performance. In no time, it seemed, he turned onto Foxhall Road, one of DC's most prestigious addresses, and less than one city block from his house on Reservoir Road.

The street lamps of the Northwest quarter had been freshly painted, and the cherry trees that lined the fashionable street were in full bloom. Even though the area was only minutes from the bustle of the Capital City, its stately single-family residences with their grassy front lawns and blacktop driveways were more akin to an upscale suburban neighborhood than an urban metropolis.

Glancing at the dashboard, he noticed that the digital clock read 10:59 p.m. It was Adam's usual style to suggest they stop in Georgetown for a quick drink and a late night snack at one of the neighborhood's trendy cafes. The bustling downtown district was a popular hangout for college coeds from Georgetown University and its sister school Mount Vernon College, and it was one of the main reasons that Adam had purchased his home in the adjacent Palisades section.

Residents of his upscale neighborhood considered it a luxury to live minutes away from the city's coolest shopping district, and at the same time, be surrounded by beautiful homes with multi-car garages and ample backyards. But, it was getting late and he and Athena decided to call it a night.

Passing the intersection of Kenmore Street, Adam stepped gingerly on his brake, in order to make a slow turn onto Reservoir Road. But the sight of flashing red lights, and the shadowy figure of a uniformed policeman directing him to stop, startled him. Scanning the scene, he saw wide swaths of blazing yellow "CRIME SCENE" tapes roped across the busy two-lane avenue. Since moving to the neighborhood nearly five years before, Adam had never once seen a policeman in the area and he found the presence of the officer and the barrier itself both frightening and ominous. Reaching for the electric control, he opened the driver's side window. "What's going on, officer?" Adam directed his question to a brawny policeman who was standing near a patrol car parked diagonally across the road, its roof aswirl with red alert lights.

Visions of a terrorist takeover filled the thirty-something attorney's mind as he watched the sinewy, dark-haired officer nearing the Toyota. He had often wondered about the ramifications of purchasing a home so close to the German Embassy and had even played out several Tom Clancy scenarios in his imagination.

The fact that he lived in what law enforcement experts considered to be one of the safest sections of Washington, DC did not negate the anxiety he had each time he sighted one of the embassy's private security cars patrolling the hilly compound across the street from his own home. The ominous presence of armed guards, coupled with life in such close proximity to the White House made his concerns eminently logical to him. Now, face to face with a police blockade, Adam could not help but wonder if his wildest imaginings were not, in fact, coming true.

"This road is closed," the young patrol officer bellowed his response.

"I live here on this street," Adam yelled out the open car window. "What's happened?"

"You say you live here on this block?" the officer said. "Then why don't you go around and come up Reservoir the other way?"

It was not Adam's style to acquiesce to any demand but he deferred to the officer and obediently backed his vehicle onto Foxhall Road, notions of bomb threats and hostage negotiations coursing through his imagination.

His mind raced. He thought first of his young housemate, Carrie, a quiet suburban woman who worried constantly about the disturbing crime rate in the Capital City. Is she home yet? If not, what will she think when she returns this evening to find a full-fledged police barricade in front of her house?

Taking a right onto MacArthur Boulevard, Adam has-

tened along the sleepy residential street of low-slung apartment buildings, and obsessed about the weird and
unexplained situation now unfolding on his block.

"What do you think happened?" He turned to his girlfriend and swallowed hard.

"I can't imagine what could have happened," Athena
answered, staring straight ahead as they passed an old Navy
fortress and unobstructed views of the Reservoir on their
right. Slowing for the traffic light, they noted the employees
of the all-night gas station across the way standing on the
sidewalk, straining to view the commotion going on just up
the road.

Rounding the sharp corner, Adam and Athena were met
with flashing crimson-and-white emergency lights. Adam's
gaze was immediately drawn to the small circle of newspaper reporters assembled on the sidewalk and the thick
strips of crime scene tape secured to the hydrant just in
front of his house. Realizing that he could not gain access
to his own driveway, he quickly turned right onto a local
side street, throwing the Toyota into PARK and tugging hard
on the emergency brake to ensure that the vehicle didn't
roll down the street's steep incline and into the wire gating
that encircled the reservoir below.

Grabbing Athena's hand, the stocky young lawyer hurried back to Reservoir Road. To his alarm, he found a group
of curious onlookers standing on the pavement just in front
of his neighbor's house.

"What's going on? What happened?" he addressed anyone who might answer him.

"There's been a shooting," a young woman reporter responded.

A shooting on his block? Adam was stunned. How could
this be?

"A shooting?" he repeated loudly. "Who was shot?"

"The woman who lives in that house." She pointed her finger at the red-brick residence with the tall white pillars that was three doors down from Adam's house.

That was Jeremy Akers' place, Adam thought.

"Who did the shooting?" Adam persisted. "Was anybody killed?"

"The guy shot his wife," the reporter responded, gazing challengingly at Adam to see his reaction.

"Wife?" Adam echoed her message in a quizzical, un-comprehending tone.

He had been living almost next door to this guy for nearly five years, had watched him jog up and down the street dozens of times, had peered out the window at him on countless afternoons to see him riding bikes with his two young kids. He had *never* seen him with a woman, and had had no idea that he was even married. Adam had just assumed that he was another of the burgeoning numbers of single dads he knew who were raising their kids alone be-cause they were either widowed or divorced.

When he had spoken briefly to Jeremy several months before during a casual sidewalk encounter—the first con-versation they had ever had in five years of living three doors away from each other—Adam remembered that their discussion sort of turned him off. He didn't care much for the "manner" of the genteel-toned but rigidly opinionated Southern gentleman.

"He shot his wife. In front of the kids," the voice of a baritone newspaper reporter pronounced dispassionately, interrupting Adam's recollection.

"In front of the kids?" Adam squeezed Athena's hand as he echoed the gruesome news.

"Did they take him into custody?" Adam asked, not be-lieving what he was hearing.

"Where are the kids now?" Athena interrupted.

"They're with a neighbor," the reporter responded, ┊ voice nearly drowned out by the crackle of the two-way radio on the dashboard of the nearby police cruiser.

"They don't know where the guy is," a second reporter delivered the shocking news. "He shot her, and then he jumped into his truck and took off."

The thought of Jeremy driving around the city with a loaded firearm sent a shiver through Adam's body.

"Which neighbor has the children?" Athena queried, watching as the female reporter raised her arm and pointed to the house directly to the right of the crime scene. The rambling red-brick home that the reporter referred to resembled Jeremy's house, save for the pricey hand-painted tiles that decorated its front steps.

That's Peter and Christy's house, Adam thought. He knew that the families shared a common driveway and that Peter and his wife had children of similar ages to the Akers kids. He even remembered hearing something about all of their kids attending the same private school.

The scene inside Peter's house must be insufferable, Adam imagined, unable to reconcile the emotional state of the two young Akers children witnessing their father shooting their mother and then watching him take off in a frenzied rage.

Even more frightening was the idea that this madman was armed and driving through the city, bent on who knew what kind of destruction.

CHAPTER TWO

THE RING OF THE TELEPHONE SHATTERED THE STILLNESS of the night. Bill Ranger sat up abruptly in bed, and took a moment to get his bearings. It wasn't that late, just about 11:30, but he had turned in unusually early—especially for a Saturday night.

It wasn't Bill's habit to answer the phone, so as usual he let the machine pick up. Too many times the caller turned out to be an old girlfriend making one last attempt at reining in the confirmed bachelor. The fifty-two-year-old Navy reservist sat in the dark and listened for a while, not really wanting to get out of bed and still hazy from the deep sleep that had enveloped him. But the familiar baritone at the other end of the line startled him into full alertness, especially when he heard the words, "I want to be buried at Arlington Cemetery."

Throwing off the covers, he sprang out of bed and picked up the receiver. By the time he crossed the room, the machine had recorded a solid minute of the frantic diatribe.

"Akers!" Ranger barked into the phone. "What are you talking about?"

"I shot Nancy."

His friend's words hit him like a fist in the chest. His first reaction was that what he was hearing couldn't possibly be true.

"This is a really bad joke," Ranger declared.

Even as he said the words, his stomach tightened. He knew perfectly well that Jeremy Akers wasn't one to kid around.

For twenty years, Bill Ranger and Jeremy Akers had traveled in the same circles, attending the same parties and socializing with the same people. A mutual friend had introduced them more than twenty years before. As soon as Jeremy learned that Bill had served as an enlisted navy seal in Vietnam, he decided to count him among his select group of friends. As far as Jeremy was concerned, there were two kinds of people: those who had served their country and those who hadn't. Ranger always found Jeremy to be a real black-and-white kind of guy. Either he liked you, or he didn't, and he made no bones about telling you if he didn't. When talking about Jeremy, four words immediately came to Ranger's mind: *intense, discerning, critical*, and *loyal*.

"No, I'm serious," Akers insisted in the same low-pitched tone, his Alabama drawl still thick even after twenty years in Washington, DC. "I killed Nancy. I shot her."

Hearing Nancy Richards Akers' name made his stomach clench even more. While he and Akers had been friends for two decades, Bill had met the woman who had become his friend's wife even earlier. He had been studying at Georgetown University, attending the Foreign Service school, when he first met the pretty, dark-haired Mt. Vernon College coed. She was a regular at Clyde's of Georgetown, a popular tavern frequented by students from both schools, and the place where Bill was employed as a waiter on a part-time basis. He remembered that she often stopped in after Sunday brunch to pick up her roommate, a hostess at the M Street eatery whom he had dated for a short time. It had been a surprising coincidence when his new friend Akers showed up at a party with his young bride and

Ranger discovered that he already knew her.

Jeremy and Nancy had been introduced while they were both working on Capitol Hill—he as a lawyer for the Justice Department, she as a speechwriter for a US Congressman, Sam Ervin of North Carolina. Both of them had energetically pursued their careers, with Jeremy becoming a respected environmental attorney who traveled all over the country investigating Superfund toxic waste cleanup sites and oil spills, and Nancy dazzling the publishing world with her success as an author of more than a dozen steamy romance novels.

While Ranger was extremely fond of them both, he had always been struck by how well the couple demonstrated the old saying, "Opposites attract." He saw Nancy as a bohemian, sweet and nurturing but with a delightful sense of style. Yet her free-spiritedness belied her roots as a society girl who had even "debuted" at a coming-out party thrown by her blueblood grandparents. Jeremy, meanwhile, came from modest means. While he loved his family, and returned home to Alabama often, Ranger noted that he clearly preferred that part of his life to be unknown. He did not want to be thought of as the "good old boy" from the South, preferring instead to be recognized as a graduate of the University of Virginia's School of Law, and a successful DC attorney.

Jeremy was completely fearless, and as a young man, he hunted alligators for sport. He had been decorated for valor in Vietnam, receiving the Silver Star—the third highest honor bestowed on a Marine. Nancy was the soft-spoken peacemaker, while Jeremy would fight to the end if he believed he was right—even if it meant putting himself and others in danger.

But as someone who had never married, Ranger felt he was in no position to judge the suitability of the pair. Besides, he had spent a great deal of time with the Akerses over the years, and had always found them to be compatible, at least as far as he could see.

Still finding his friend's whole bizarre admission difficult to believe, he decided to shift gears.

"Okay, Akers," he said, hoping that his matter-of-fact tone would bring out "the real truth," which he expected would be a repudiation of the grisly confession. "What did you do—and how long ago?"

"About thirty minutes ago," Jeremy replied dryly.

The conversation was beginning to feel surreal to Bill. But slowly he was coming around to believing that his buddy could actually be speaking the truth.

A vision of what might have happened began forming in his mind. He knew that Nancy had left her family, and that Jeremy had been devastated by the fact that she quickly moved in with another man more than twenty years his junior. The fact that the interloper was a truck driver— someone Jeremy considered beneath both him and his wife, and a bad influence on his children—had caused his anger to escalate into rage. Nevertheless, Ranger believed that Akers had found a way to deal with the trauma. Nancy had left him the previous October, and it was now June 5, 1999.

He remembered the day his friend had broken the news to him. It was just like any other day when "Popeye"—his nickname for Akers because of the former Marine's compact, muscular frame—flagged him down.

Ranger assumed that, as usual, Akers was looking for a jogging partner. Instead, the look on his face immediately told him something else was up.

Akers leaned into the car so that his face was a few inches away from Ranger's. It was one of his habits that most people found disconcerting—that, and the gold eye tooth that Jeremy was so proud of. "Nancy left me," he said.

Ranger could see how broken Jeremy was as he spewed forth his frustration and anger. But most prominent was his utter disbelief. "No one leaves me," he growled.

That had been eight months earlier, and while he had talked about it obsessively, Ranger just presumed that Jeremy was finding a way to deal with it.

Now, faced with this bizarre admission, Ranger began to wonder whether Akers really had killed Nancy. He imagined a scenario at the cramped one-bedroom apartment that Nancy and her new lover Jim had taken together—ironically, just a few blocks away from the elegant red-brick Federal-style house in which Jeremy and Nancy had lived for nearly fifteen years of their marriage.

"What'd you do, go down to the apartment?" Ranger asked, choosing his words cautiously.

"No, no. It was in front of the house, and I'm only sorry that I didn't get *him*."

Ranger knew immediately to whom he was referring.

"I wanted to get them together, and I'm disappointed that I couldn't."

"I shot her in front of the house," he continued, his voice unwavering as he described the macabre scenario to his friend. "She was in the car."

Suddenly another thought popped into Ranger's mind. "Where were the kids?"

"On the front steps of the porch," Jeremy replied.

Ranger's heart stopped. "You've got to be kidding me."

Like everybody else who knew him, Ranger knew how much Jeremy adored his two sons, Finny and Zeb, and his daughter, Isabelle. He took them everywhere with him: to the park, on hikes, to Alabama to visit his family every chance he got. Because both men's houses were in the same neighborhood, Ranger had to pass the Akers residence every time he went to what he jokingly referred to as his "blue collar Safeway." And just about every time he went by, he spotted the square-shouldered, five-foot, seven-inch former Marine on the front lawn playing with his children. If they weren't engaged in an energetic game of Frisbee, they would be romping with the family's rottweiler or climbing onto their bikes for a ride to the nearby park.

But something had gone terribly wrong.

Bill was back to thinking the whole grisly story had to be a hoax. Akers' contention that the children were on the front steps during the episode he was describing was just too out of character to be taken seriously.

In fact, he remembered Akers saying something about a hearing that was scheduled for just two weeks away. He wasn't certain, but he believed that the meeting might have been to determine the custody of the two minor children. In their twenty years of friendship, Ranger had never known Akers to be afraid of anything. The possible loss of his kids was the first thing he had ever reacted to with fear.

"Take me through this again." Ranger rubbed the tensed muscles of his forehead. "Let's start from the beginning."

"I did it down the street, with the kids on the porch," Jeremy repeated in the same matter-of-fact tone.

"That's just incredible—that you did it in front of the kids."

"This is a very bad joke," Ranger finally declared after the conversation had continued for close to twenty minutes. He still hoped that his friend was making up a story, but his attitude slowly shifted from one of shock and denial to a more somber, contemplative state. For a moment he was silent, as he struggled to imagine what could have possibly triggered such an extreme reaction.

"She left me, and I cannot take that she left me," Akers told his friend in a deep, prosaic voice. "In the car tonight, I was trying to give her another chance, and she said no."

A hundred conversations that he had had with Akers replayed in Ranger's mind. For months, during their frequent fifteen-mile jogs around the nearby reservoir, he had listened to Akers' tirades against his wife. Her abandonment of him, especially for another man, went against the grain of everything he believed in as a religious Christian, raised in a backwoods northern Alabama town where traditional values were revered. The culture that had shaped Jeremy remained very much a part of him. Ranger knew that his friend was finding it impossible to come to terms with an unfaithful wife.

"Akers, you're scaring me. Did you really do this?" Ranger persisted, his shock turning to anger. "Your ego got in the way. Think about Zeb and Isabelle. What's going to happen to them?"

Everything, he realized, was out of control. Akers was talking from an upside-down world. If he'd killed his wife in front of the kids, what was he going to do next? Jeremy was a loose cannon, and this scared even the calm, cool Ranger.

"Please let me come and get you," Ranger pleaded. "Where are you?"

Akers' reply made his blood run cold. "It's too late. I'm not going to jail. I'm going on a new and different voyage."

"I think you're probably insane at this stage, and that you can plead insanity," Ranger retorted.

"As an attorney," Jeremy replied calmly, "I know that wouldn't work."

"Let me come get you," Ranger insisted. "Just tell me where you are."

When Akers refused to answer, Ranger tried a different tack. "What's going to happen to the kids?"

"The neighbors will take care of them." Akers was referring to a couple who lived next door to him on Reservoir

Road. "I just hope what I've done doesn't upset Chrissy."

"Chrissy?" Ranger was puzzled. Who the devil was he talking about?

"The neighbor's wife," Akers responded. "She's eight months pregnant. I hope that what I've done doesn't have a negative impact on the baby."

Ranger was speechless. That his friend would now be concerned about his neighbor's unborn child was difficult to fathom, given what he had just admitted.

"I'm going to give you my parents' number," Akers continued. "But don't call them, because they're old."

Now that Jeremy had mentioned his family, Ranger realized he didn't know how many brothers and sisters his friend had. But Akers had thought of that, too.

"I have an older brother and a younger sister," Akers explained. "W. T. and Carolyn."

"Where are your medals and your service jacket?" Ranger asked.

"If you can get into the house," he replied, "there's an envelope upstairs with twenty-eight hundred dollars in cash for the kids. And speaking of the kids, I'm counting on you to explain it to them, and tell them that I love them." Ranger could hear the tone of his friend's voice soften when he mentioned the children.

Somberly Jeremy added, "I love my country, but I just couldn't live with the shame of my wife leaving me."

Then Akers repeated the words that he had said to his friend many times, that he wanted to be buried at Arlington. Ranger listened intently. He waited. He wanted more information. Mirroring Akers' calm tone, the decorated naval officer decided to be strategic. "Okay, Akers, I'll honor your request, but where do I find the body?" Ranger inquired, thinking that if his friend were close by, he could reach him before it was too late.

But Jeremy replied, "I'm not going to tell you. I don't want to give you that responsibility."

Ranger said once again, "Let me come pick you up."

He could tell immediately that Akers was becoming anxious.

"I have to go and take care of business."

"Jeremy, I am begging you not to do this. And I don't beg for anything."

He hoped that showing his urgency might work more effectively than the other ploys he had tried.

"You're a good friend, Ranger," Akers said. "I've got to go."

As Ranger started begging him once again to listen to reason, he heard his friend say, "Goodbye."

The next thing he heard was a dial tone.

Frantically, Ranger pressed *-6-9 on his cordless phone. His heart crumpled when he didn't recognize the number that he was given, especially since the 202 area code indicated that Jeremy was close by, calling from somewhere inside Washington.

Ranger punched in 9-1-1.

A woman's voice answered. "Nine-one-one. Where is your emergency?"

"A friend of mine I believe just killed his wife and is about to kill himself," Ranger reported, struggling to keep his voice in control. "Here's the number where he's calling from."

"What's his address?" the operator asked methodically.

Intense frustration rose inside Ranger like a wave. Trying to get cooperation from her, he thought, was like pulling teeth out of a hen. "No, he's not calling from home. He's calling from this number, and if you can trace this number right away, you might be able to find him."

"Fine. Thanks."

When he heard the click that told him she had hung up, his level of annoyance reached unbearable levels. Still clutching the receiver of the cordless Sony, he ran through his house to the driveway.

He leaped into his car, and sped the quarter of a mile from his own home to Jeremy's, on the same street. Reservoir Road was an unlikely place for a crime to be committed. It was the home of several embassies, including the French Embassy and the German Embassy. While the police respected the wishes of the well-heeled residents and made a point of not being an obvious presence, they were vigilant about maintaining order in this high-profile section of the District of Columbia.

"I know Akers is not a bullshit kind of guy," he thought, grimly gripping the wheel. "Maybe there's a chance, a four-point-two percent chance, that this didn't happen."

But as he neared the Akerses' elegant red-brick residence, the flicker of emergency lights told him otherwise.

Reservoir Road was entirely blocked off. Police cars were lined up, blocking the street so that no one could approach the house. The emergency lights, whirling from the roofs, cast an eerie glow over the posh neighborhood. The uniformed cops and plainclothes detectives milling around were a peculiar contrast to the dignified German Embassy directly across the street from his friend's house.

The drama of the scene was heightened by the fact that the embassy had set up its own barricade. The extensive stretch of property that housed the modern, multileveled building was shielded from the street by a tall, forbidding iron fortress. It was considered foreign soil, and uniformed German security personnel armed with sub-machine guns had been ordered to create a barricade in front of the chancellery. They, too, had heard the shots, and their immediate response had been to go into high alert mode and defend the foreign embassy in case the shooting turned out to be a security threat. Ranger suddenly felt as if he'd been cat-apulted into a Fellini film.

He knew immediately that the worst was true. Akers had done the unthinkable. He really *had* murdered his wife.

Metropolitan Police Sergeant Michael Farish had been less than a half-mile away, patrolling the fashionable streets of downtown Georgetown, when the emergency call, "Shots fired!" crackled over his radio. Glancing at the digital clock on the car's dashboard, he had noted that it was exactly 10:27 p.m.

"Units respond to the 4600 block of Reservoir Road," the disembodied voice of the police dispatcher broadcast the location as Farish reached down to switch on his siren.

"On it!" The thirty-nine-year-old detective grabbed the mike and shouted into the handset. He had been on Wis-consin Avenue heading north back toward the stationhouse, winding down now that there were less than forty minutes left on his evening tour. He knew that the broadcast was directed at patrol unit officers, but the nature of the call, and the fact that the incident had occurred in his district while he was the officer in charge, cued him to respond.

Pressing hard on the brake of his Ford Crown Victoria, he jerked the steering wheel of his unmarked car, its tires screeching. He flicked on the whirling red bubble light mounted atop the dashboard, hung a sharp left, and accel-erated west in the direction of Reservoir Road.

The veteran investigator already had a sense that this call was going to turn out to be more than a routine run. It wasn't every day that the words "Shots fired" came across the radio, at least not for this location. While too many of Washington, DC's neighborhoods were riddled with crime, the posh Palisades section of Georgetown was rarely the scene of any crimes more threatening than jaywalking. A call like this was bound to draw a considerable amount of attention from the higher-ups in his department—not to mention the media.

Farish pressed his foot on the gas and heard a second message crackle over his radio. "Child, eleven years old, is in the house alone," the disembodied voice announced.

"Oh, God, please not the kid, you jerk," he thought.

Veering onto Reservoir Road, the sergeant caught up and tucked his vehicle in behind a uniformed patrol car that was heading to the scene. With a practiced eye he scanned the idyllic scene, with its manicured lawns and neatly trimmed shrubs, as he looked for signs of disturbance. His attention was immediately drawn to the fire trucks that were stopped halfway up the block, pulled up next to a late model Jeep Wrangler. The vehicle was facing in an easterly direction on the south side of the busy two-lane street.

Parking behind the polished white patrol car with its official red stripes, the seasoned investigator wrenched his lanky, six-foot, two-inch frame from the vehicle and hurried toward the Jeep. He immediately recognized the officer in the first car as Sergeant Christopher Saunders of the Special Operations Division, the arm of the Metropolitan Police Department responsible for presidential matters such as motorcades, as well as crowd control at parades and demonstrations. He noted that Saunders was still in uniform. Only later did he learn that he had just gone off-duty and was on his way home when he picked up the "radio run," the department's official term for an emergency call, on the Second District's radio channel.

Sirens wailed from the fire trucks and emergency medical units that had stopped alongside the Jeep as Farish moved in for a closer look. He could see that its parking lights were still on, and that the driver's side door hung open. The overhead street lamp illuminated the Wrangler's out-of-state license plate, Illinois D810-198—and the body that was slumped in the driver's seat, leaning toward the passenger side.

The lifeless form was dressed in a navy-and-white striped sleeveless tee-shirt and baggy black slacks. Silver bangle bracelets encircled her motionless arms. Her thick, wavy dark hair had fallen over her face, concealing it from view. Farish surveyed the spectacle with a dispassion that was the result of seventeen years on the Metropolitan Police Department. He had moved to the District of Columbia from Philadelphia as a young boy when his father was transferred to the Naval Annex across the street from the Pentagon, and at twenty-one, joined the police force as a patrol officer in the Third District. After receiving a promotion to the rank of sergeant, Farish was transferred to the Central Homicide unit.

While there, he was called to the scenes of hundreds of murders, spectacles so grisly they caused him to recoil in horror. In a city that at one time was known for handling between three hundred and four hundred murders a year, Farish witnessed on a daily basis what few men viewed even once in a lifetime. Cases like the toddler who was killed by a blow to the head with a hammer, and the elderly woman who had been beaten to death for her welfare check had taught him to compartmentalize the job. He had learned to view dead bodies not as people, but as another piece of evidence to help solve the crime.

Instinctively he began to piece together what had happened. There was so much he didn't know about the case. Had the gunman shot the woman from the sidewalk? Had this incident been a drive-by shooting? Did it have anything to do with the German Embassy across the street?

He knew two things perfectly well: that you never know

what you have, and that you always anticipate the worst. To counterbalance his doubts, he also had two decades of experience in one of the nation's homicide capitals to draw upon. He had been trained at Basic Investigator School within the department, in an advanced homicide program in Baltimore, and also at the prestigious Harvard Associates in Police Science in Virginia.

Now, as he watched the emergency medical technician struggle to pull the woman from the vehicle, he could not help but think that there was nothing anyone could do to maximize the possibility that the outcome of this crime would be positive. There was no question that she was dead.

Farish focused on the blood that drenched the passenger seat of the vehicle, still so fresh it was a brilliant red. Two puncture marks on the left side of the victim's head signified that two shots had been fired. The absence of stippling, a burn ring left by gunfire, indicated to him that the assailant had fired from close range. He could see that the lower portion of her left earlobe was missing, and gray brain matter, intermingled with blood, lay in clumps in her thick, wavy, dark hair.

Despite the fact that this woman was clearly dead, the EMT workers were busily attempting to resuscitate her. They pulled the oxygen tanks down from the fire truck, and placed the ambu bag over her face as they launched into basic CPR. He watched the technician insert a tube into the victim's airway.

"This is CR 200." The detective overheard the technician reporting his findings to the dispatcher, who would record the call in the official police file next to the time, 22:39:35. "Be advised, victim is in serious condition."

He could see that there was movement in her chest and stomach each time the medic squeezed the bag, but observed no noticeable signs of breath. Farish knew that once bagging and compressing the victim failed to produce any results, additional medical personnel would arrive on the scene to load the body onto the bright orange gurney and transport it via ambulance to nearby Georgetown Hospital.

"Block it off!" the sergeant shouted to the uniformed officers pulling up to the scene. "Stop your cars, and shut it down!

"Secure the scene!" He continued to bark his orders, this time speaking into his handheld Motorola radio. His announcement would be broadcast over the Second District's official police channel and would be heard by every officer in the precinct.

"Move it back!" he snapped, noting with chagrin that the media had already started arriving and were swarming around the premises.

Farish proceeded to instruct the officer standing closest to him, dressed in the department's regulation light blue shirt and navy slacks, to secure a large section of the block. He was well versed in the area of crime-scene management. Experience had taught him that it was important to begin by roping off a sizeable area around a crime scene to ensure that detectives had ample space to conduct their investigation. He chose to have the tape placed in such a way as to rope off seventy-five to a hundred yards, keeping the gathering crowd as far away as possible.

"Make it big. I don't want people milling around in the crime scene, and I don't want any cars coming down here."

He knew the first twelve hours in a murder investigation required extensive manpower. There were extensive steps that needed to be taken. It was necessary to ID the victim, canvass the neighborhood in search of the perpetrator, and find witnesses and take their statements. Getting an accurate picture of what had happened demanded both time and skilled personnel.

Fortunately, he had the benefit of two shifts' worth of staff. The fact that it was eleven o'clock at night meant it was the end of the three-to-eleven tour and the beginning of the midnight shift. Investigators from both tours had converged on the stationhouse for the switchover, and were therefore available to rush to the scene. A few investigators were even summoned from their homes.

Concerned for the safety of the child that the dispatcher had reported was alone in the house, Farish immediately instructed four uniformed officers to conduct a protective sweep of the residence at 4632 Reservoir Road.

Farish knew that he was now at one of the most important parts of the investigation. Going inside the house and doing a careful search would reveal whether there were other victims, hostages, or even the perpetrator himself. Routine procedure was to enter the premises with utmost caution, going in with guns drawn and the expectation that anything could happen. In a situation like this, it was possible that the shooter was still nearby, hiding in a closet or crouching in a corner of a darkened room ready to strike again.

The uniformed officers cautiously climbed the brick steps to the front door. Their guns drawn, the men entered the darkened house through the front door, which had been left open. After only five minutes, one of the men emerged. "House is empty!" he announced.

Satisfied that the important first steps were being taken, and anxious to find the eleven-year-old boy who, minutes earlier, had phoned 911 for help, Farish turned to the three people who had been flagging down the police and other emergency personnel as they arrived on the scene.

"Any witnesses?" Sgt. Farish inquired.

One of them stepped forward, a man in his mid to late thirties.

"It must have been a quarter past ten when I heard what sounded like firecrackers, two explosions, a higher pitch, then a cherry bomb. Almost instantaneously I heard one of the kids crying. I went to the window and I could hear one of the kids saying, 'I love you, Daddy.' They were crying out after him.

"I opened the window further, and I could see Jeremy getting into the car that was parked on the street."

"Jeremy?" Sgt. Farish repeated.

"Jeremy Akers. He lives right there."

"Go on," Farish urged.

"He slams the door and drives off very fast, east on Reservoir Road," the man continued, adding that his next-door neighbor was driving a large SUV with Alabama license plates. "Then I thought about it a minute, that he would not be leaving his kids in distress. I thought something had to be wrong. I walked up the sidewalk in front of Akers' house. I was trying to see if there was a smell of gunpowder from the firecracker. The crying had stopped. I didn't see anybody, so I called up to see if everything was okay. There was no response, so I hesitated and I was getting ready to go back to my house when I saw Halsey and a friend of his." He gestured toward one of the other neighbors standing at the edge of the crime scene.

"So I turned to speak to them about this," he went on. "Then they turned and went back to their house. Somewhere in there, I noticed Nancy's car was parked in front of Danny's house.* So I thought she must be in the house

---

*"Danny" is a pseudonym for the neighbor, who wished to remain anonymous.

with the kids, and Jeremy stormed out of the house because of her presence.

"Then I noticed the brake lights in back of the car were on. I thought she left her lights on. I didn't see any lights on in the front. So I walked over to talk to Danny and he was preoccupied by something. So I walked up to the two to ask if they had heard the two sounds and to see if everything's okay. And I was preparing to go with him up to his house to speak to him about the events in private.

"Then I looked to the left toward the Jeep, and I believe I saw the passenger door open and there's a lump. I hoped it wasn't a person. Then I heard Danny say that it was Nancy, so I said, 'Is she responsive?'

"I called to her from the passenger side. She was slumped over, so I went around the Jeep to the driver's side and opened the door. Her left arm was propped behind her. It was propped against the steering wheel. I tried to take her pulse. I couldn't feel one, but I'm no expert at taking them.

"I rushed around the steps to their door. I passed Halsey to ask if he called an ambulance. I asked if they had given him any advice on what to do and he said that they had already called 911.

"When I got to the front door, Danny was on the phone, trying to get Homicide. Prior to that, he and his friend were taking towels down to stop the bleeding. . . .

"Then the police arrived. Just then, my wife came running up the sidewalk from our house. We'd been so focused on the Jeep we hadn't done anything about the kids. My wife was distraught. She began to worry about the kids. She then went up to the house to see if they were okay. She then came down the steps with the kids. We were in tears."

Ranger, meanwhile, had just recovered from his initial

shock upon arriving at the crime scene. He remembered the promise he had made to his friend. He had agreed to see the children, to try to explain to them what had happened.

He moved cautiously toward the house. He'd only gone a few feet when he spotted the yellow tape printed with "CRIME SCENE—DO NOT CROSS" stretched across the busy two-lane roadway. If that hadn't been enough to stop him, the two uniformed cops who stepped in his path were.

"Sorry, sir. This is a crime scene," one of them explained. "You can't go any further."

Reaching for the electric control, Ranger opened the driver's side window. "I have some information." He directed his statement at the brawny officer standing beside a shiny white patrol car parked diagonally across the road, its roof aswirl with red lights. Reaching into his pocket, he pulled a military identification card from his wallet. He flashed it at the officer, hoping it would convince him that he wasn't just some curious onlooker.

One of the officers stepped closer to the car and nodded an "okay" at Ranger as he studied the ID.

"I got a call from my friend," Ranger explained, his heart pounding as he struggled to speak clearly but still convey the urgency of the situation. "He may have killed his wife. If you can trace this number you might be able to find him."

The two officers exchanged glances.

"Wait here," the first officer ordered.

Ranger watched as one of the cops crossed the lawn, then spoke in a low voice to a tall, lean man in street attire. As he watched, he realized that he was a plainclothes investigator, most likely directing the police investigation now underway.

Ranger couldn't help being struck by the contrast between the uniformed policemen swarming the property, walkie-talkies squawking, and flickering lights casting spooky red shadows along the dimly lit street, and the dignified house that had suddenly and bizarrely been cast in the role of "scene of the crime." The elegant, two-story house, he knew, was easily worth half a million dollars.

Ranger squared his shoulders as he noticed the officer coming back his way. This time, the plainclothes detective was in tow.

"I'm Mike Farish," announced the investigator, who was dressed in impeccably pressed slacks, a crisp white shirt, and a stylish necktie. His light brown hair was cut short, and a thin mustache gave him a serious, dignified appearance. He extended his hand, and Ranger was struck by the firmness of his handshake. "I'm from the detectives' office. I understand you were called by Jeremy Akers."

Ranger held up the tiny piece of paper on which he had scribbled the phone number and handed it to the investigator. He launched into a description of the disturbing midnight phone call he had just received from Akers. Struggling to control his voice, even as he felt like exploding, he tried not to let himself get distracted by all the activity around him. Officers from the mobile crime scene unit were snapping pictures and collecting evidence. Neighbors congregated on the sidewalk, speaking in hushed tones and respectfully observing the flimsy barrier created by the yellow plastic CRIME SCENE strips.

As he spoke, Ranger was painfully aware that the clock was ticking. Every second that passed made it less likely that Jeremy Akers would be found. He kept his report as concise as he could, then handed the detective the piece of scrap paper with the scribbled phone number, hoping that the information might save his friend's life.

Sergeant Farish nodded his thanks and started back toward the crime scene.

Ranger only hesitated a moment before calling after him, "If you find him, be careful. He's determined to kill himself."

CHAPTER THREE

SERGEANT MICHAEL FARISH STOOD ON THE SIDEWALK and deliberately punched in the phone number that Bill Ranger had just handed to him. He realized that he was taking a gamble by making the call, but he decided that there wasn't time to consider the less risky alternative. He knew that his only other option would be to phone the number in to the investigator he had stationed at the precinct house, and hope that Cole's reverse telephone directory would reveal the man's location. But that could take several minutes, and there was no guarantee that the method would yield an address. He only hoped he would be able to track him down before the former Marine took his rampage to the next level and harmed somebody else. Experience had taught him that a man in Jeremy Akers' shoes, someone who has just shot and killed his wife in front of his children, was in a state of complete desperation, no longer believing there was anything else to live for.

The scenarios that were likely to follow, he knew only too well, were dismally bleak. One was for the killer to decide to go out in a blaze of glory, taking others with him. In this instance, hostages or other innocent bystanders often got caught up in a game they had never intended to play.

Another alternative was one he knew intimately. In fact, it was a horror he had lived with every day of his life for the past twelve years. Desperadoes such as Jeremy were sometimes too cowardly to take their own lives, even after taking the lives of others. In those instances, they often chose what in the police world was known as a "suicide by cop."

In his own case, the lanky, 192-pound officer had been called to the scene of a drug deal gone awry. When he arrived at the location, he found a narcotics dealer holding a gun to the head of a security guard.

"Drop the weapon!" he had yelled in an effort to diffuse the situation, drawing his gun from his holster.

There was no response. Instead, the crazed gunman had pressed the barrel even closer to the innocent guard's head.

"Drop it!" Farish tried again, instinctively gripping his gun even more tightly.

In a sudden motion, the dealer had turned the weapon toward Farish and the other officers on the scene. The security guard jumped away as Farish fired once, killing the desperate gunman.

Later, it was discovered that the gun the dealer had been brandishing was a realistic-looking toy—so real, in fact, that a Grand Jury could not differentiate it from the real thing. That moment had stayed with him, and his worst fear was that one of his own officers would be put in a similar situation and have to spend the rest of his career reliving the memory, as he had.

Farish glanced at his watch. He realized that over an hour had passed since Jeremy Akers had killed his wife. A hundred different possibilities of what could be happening at that very moment raced through his mind—each one worse than the last. While Jeremy had most likely shot his wife in a moment of passion, the ensuing hour had no doubt given him time for the significance of what he had done to sink in—and a chance for him to realize that no matter what action he took, he was destined to spend the rest of his life in prison.

To Farish's way of thinking, a man killing his wife in front of the kids was about as low as anyone could get. From what he had learned about Akers, with his Marine background as a trained killer and his macho attitudes, he feared that his mindset was, "You'll never catch me; I'm a survivor." He could envision the next step being a high-speed chase, with Akers popping off a few rounds to make good his escape.

He also knew there was another player who was likely to get drawn into this grotesque drama. In the past hour, his investigation had revealed that Nancy Richards-Akers had a lover—a man who could very well be the next name on Jeremy Akers' hit list.

Sgt. Farish was relieved to learn that the youngsters were safe inside the neighbor's home, and that the young man's wife was caring for them.

Farish knew immediately what the next step was—to interview the children. But first, he needed to send out an All Points Bulletin to alert police departments in the region to the gunman on the loose. Reaching into his pocket, the sergeant retrieved his radio and called up the communications supervisor.

"We need an All Units Simulcast," he declared, instructing the dispatcher to send out notification to every officer in the District of Columbia, as well as headquarters of every police station along much of the eastern seaboard to be on the lookout for Jeremy Akers.

It was exactly 22:42:01 on June 5, 1999, when the radio broadcast went over the airwaves: "All units, be on the lookout for white male, five foot, seven inches, bangs, muscular build, possibly driving a dark colored Ford Expedition . . . He is considered armed and dangerous."

CHAPTER FOUR

JEREMY AKERS CLUTCHED THE STEERING WHEEL OF HIS coal-black Mercury Mountaineer, the thick muscles of his forearms bulging from the intensity of his grip. Thoughts of his wife and her live-in boyfriend raced through his mind as he headed for 4840 MacArthur Boulevard. Methodically, he drove the dimly lit streets of the quiet, tree-lined neighborhood in search of a secluded spot to park his vehicle and begin his hunt for his second target, Jim Lemke.

Nancy could have saved her own life, Jeremy rationalized as he drove along, replaying the final conversation with his estranged wife over and over in his mind.

Her arrogant, flat-out refusal to leave her young lover and come back to him had proved too infuriating for him to bear. Didn't she realize that he could no longer live with the shame and embarrassment he felt each time that he thought of her with that low-life, 18-wheeler jerk?

Things between them had been so different, he recalled, remembering when Nancy had made him feel like the center of the universe.

Jeremy first met the shapely brunette more than twenty years before when they had both been working on Capitol Hill. A mutual friend had introduced the couple, believing they were perfectly matched. In reality, they couldn't have been more different.

*　　*　　*

Born in Mississippi on April 1, 1942, Jeremy Ray was the first son of William and Gladys Akers. Nicknamed "Jerry Ray" by his family, the adorable, fair-haired boy with the piercing blue eyes and deep voice moved with his family to Sheffield, Alabama, where his father worked for the powerful Southern Railway System. The small industrial town, which sits seventy miles west of Huntsville in the northwest corner of the state, is where he would spend all of his youth.

Named for its sister city of Sheffield, England, Jeremy's hometown was incorporated in 1885 amid speculation of a land boom in the region known as The Shoals. A trading post, Sheffield was actually developed in 1816 by a group of land speculators, including generals Andrew Jackson and John Coffee. However, the undertaking was soon abandoned in favor of Florence on the opposite bank of the river.

While most towns in the South were developed as agricultural centers that were helped by gradual and steady growth of the economy, Sheffield was founded by a handful of entrepreneurs who invested their fortunes to build a city with industries from which they hoped to earn a profit. Their plan was to create an iron and steel center using locally available iron ore and to capitalize on the economy of river transportation to ship the product to market. The demand for iron had created a need for production sites near the areas where iron ore was plentiful, and by the turn of the century, five blast furnaces were in operation along the banks of the Tennessee River.

Wide streets, brick sidewalks, and sprawling industrial plants characterized Jerry Ray's hometown, one of four towns collectively referred to as the "Quad-Cities." Florence, the largest of the four, sits on the south side of the river and has the biggest commercial district. While Sheffield had just one movie house, Florence had two, making the more populated city a desirable destination for the area's teen population.

When Jeremy—or *Jerry* as he was referred to by the local folk—was born, the provincial Southern community had a population of fewer than eight thousand people and a crime rate that was virtually non-existent—save for "the occasional husband killing his wife," local folks like to joke.

Jerry enjoyed two short years as an only child before sharing the spotlight with his new brother, William Thomas Akers, Jr., or "T" as his family called him. Three years later, a sister, Carolyn, was born. Jeremy's parents mused about the little girl's bony, bird-like frame, and lovingly nicknamed her "Chicken." It was a name that would stick with her, even after she won the title of "homecoming queen" of her senior class, and became a wife and mother herself.

As a youngster, Jerry was keenly aware that something important was happening in the world. His first indication was the day his father, a proud and private man, was sent overseas to defend his country in World War II as a member of the United States Marines Corps. Everywhere Jerry went, he heard talk of the teenage sons of neighbors joining the fight, and he watched as members of his close-knit community traded items such as shirts and shoes for sugar and other rationed goods.

Military service had always been an important piece of the Akers family heritage. Everybody in town knew that Jerry's great-great uncle on his mother's side was Albert Sidney Johnston, who led his troops in a notorious battle of the War Between the States. Growing up, Jerry's parents proudly educated their son and his siblings about the host of relatives who had served as generals and colonels in the conflicts of the South.

Because of the proximity of the Wilson Dam and the nearby industrial plants that were turning out critical war materials, the Akers children were members of a community that the government had declared a "sensitive" region. Fearing attacks from the Germans to the east and the Japanese to the west, blackout drills and the construction of air raid shelters in The Shoals started even before Jerry's siblings were born.

With many of the nearby factories now operating on an around-the-clock basis, Jerry and his family watched their tiny community swell from eight thousand to more than ten thousand in just a few months. Brimming with a workforce of well-paid employees, the Quad-Cities continued to prosper even after World War II ended. The main shopping district along Montgomery Avenue bustled with patrons of its many restaurants and shops. Family-run establishments like the Sheffield Pharmacy and the Colbert Theater were popular spots for Jerry and his young friends.

The post-war economy was good not only for Sheffield, but for Jerry's dad as well, who worked as a railway laborer, while his mother remained at home to run her busy household.

Gladys Akers kept a tidy home. The attractive, well-spoken woman took pride in the boxy, five-room house that the family occupied on Nineteenth Avenue. The home was typical of the residences that dotted the oak-lined streets of their middle-class neighborhood. But unlike the neighbors' houses, which were faced with inexpensive asbestos siding, the Akers residence boasted a lovely brick façade that set it apart from others in the community.

While modest in size, Jerry's house was neatly landscaped with flowers and shrubs, and was only a stone's throw from the more exclusive section of the city. He and his friends often rode their bicycles on the broad streets that wound their way along the limestone bluffs of the Tennessee River, stopping to marvel at the impressive mansions that sat perched behind towering Pines along the banks.

Like most of the southern towns, Sheffield was segregated. The black families populated an area not far from Jerry's house that locals referred to as "Baptist Bottom." The small downtown district maintained its own churches and its own school, and the children of the black community were discouraged from socializing with those of the larger white community.

Growing up in a town that was right on the banks of the Tennessee River afforded Jerry and the other children of Sheffield the opportunity to enjoy a plethora of outdoor activities. For the oldest Akers boy, they included swimming, boating, and fishing in the summer months, as well as hiking the trails of the nearby parklands, and hunting in the woody areas near his home. From an early age, Jerry was proficient with guns and, as he grew older, he began collecting them as a hobby.

When he was in second grade, Jerry met the boy who would become his best pal. Raymond Walker and his family had moved to Sheffield from Birmingham shortly after Ray's dad left the Marine Corps. His new friend was taller and leaner than Jerry when he enrolled at Blake Elementary School, in a school system that had only eight hundred students from kindergarten to twelfth grade.

Both from modest means, and both with fathers who had served in the Marine Corps, Jerry and Ray hit it off right from the start and became inseparable. As youngsters, they rode bicycles together after school. As teens they doubledated. And, as young men, they attended Florence State

Teachers College and then enrolled at the University of Alabama, pledging the same fraternity.

Their friendship began with their membership in the Cub Scouts, which they belonged to for three years. Dressed in their official blue uniforms, they enjoyed after-school activities and weekend sleep-outs where hiking and swimming were part of the fun. While the boys were proud members of the popular club, their participation in the organization was focused more on the social enjoyment it provided, and less on the badges and patches the other boys took pride in earning for their community service.

Jerry's mom liked that her son belonged to such an upright, worthwhile club, and she volunteered to serve as a Cub Scout mother to the local troop. Her participation as a volunteer with the Cub Scouts was just one of the roles that she played as an active member of the Sheffield community. Gladys Akers belonged to a host of local organizations, the most important of which was her affiliation with the First United Methodist Church on North Montgomery Avenue. On Sundays, Gladys dressed her sons in the crisp white shirts that she painstakingly ironed, and sat proudly by her family's side as the minister gave his sermon. Often, Jerry and his family would find seating near the Walkers, since Gladys and Mrs. Walker were also good friends.

Jerry's father rarely accompanied the family to church. To Jerry's friends, William Akers was a man of few words. The former Marine was a loner. Residents of the small community described him as a typical parent of the forties and fifties, a nose-to-the-grindstone type who adhered rigidly to the traditional role of husband as breadwinner and father as rule-maker and enforcer. He was a no-nonsense parent who believed that discipline and example were more important than mushy declarations or expressions of affection. With his son, he was sometimes critical and often

remote, choosing to leave the child-rearing responsibilities—
except for punishment—in the hands of his wife.

As a seventh grader, Jerry enrolled at Sheffield Junior
High School. He was twelve years old and entering puberty,
and aware that many of his friends at the red-brick schoolhouse were experiencing growth spurts that seemed to elude
him. His best pal Ray shot up to nearly six feet tall by the
time they had completed the eighth grade, and most of the
other boys in his class had also grown markedly taller during their middle school years.

Jerry was deeply concerned when his own stature remained relatively unchanged, but stoically kept his anxiety
to himself. Such stoicism may have been one of the first
signals that Jerry repressed his deep, painful emotions, especially his feelings of inadequacy. Perhaps if he had been
more expressive about his concerns, he would have been
given support, empathy or at least an opportunity to discuss
his feelings. He began the ninth grade standing just five
feet, one inch tall, and remained that height until early in
the twelfth grade, when he finally grew seven inches. But
even then he was unable to stand shoulder to shoulder with
his classmates. His height meant that he could not participate in the traditional high school sports of football and
basketball, a fact that rankled the athletic young man. While
it was clear that he was highly intelligent, and had an I.Q.
that friends say exceeded 160, his inability to join the
school's popular athletic teams was bitterly disappointing
to the clean-cut teenager. But, determined to show his
school spirit, he supported the players he longed to join by
yelling cheers from the sidelines. His classmates voted him
one of three boys on the nine-person Sheffield Cheerleaders
team, an appointment that was considered prestigious by
members of the school population.

At weekend games, he was outfitted in the official cheerleading garb for boys: crisp white slacks, a pressed collared shirt, a bow tie around his neck, and a white Varsity-style button-down sweater with the school's "patch" sewn on its lower left pocket. The slender teen wore his hair cropped short and slicked neatly upwards, and performed a repertoire of gymnastic feats. His role included lifting and throwing the six skirt-clad, saddle-shoed girls of the squad, and performing acrobatic feats on the grassy field during half time.

Jerry's participation on the squad won him visibility at the popular sporting events, and the affections of some of the prettiest girls in his class. On weekends, he and Ray kept a busy schedule, double-dating their sweethearts at drive-in movies and the bowling alley that had recently opened in Sheffield. Alcohol was not popular among members of the Sheffield teen community, and Jerry and Ray never touched a drink until they left home for college.

For the most part, Jerry preferred to date girls from neighboring Florence High School, and rarely, if ever, took out any of the women from his own alma mater. His friends recall that he never really had a steady girlfriend, but rarely was without a date on a Saturday night.

Jerry was a member of more clubs than most of his classmates joined, maintaining a social life that was the envy of many of the boys in his class. He served all four years as a member of the Student Council, and amassed a list of accomplishments that included everything from manager of the school's basketball team to Class President. He held the title of "Class Favorite" student for four years in a row, and also counted membership in the Honor Society and Key Club among his many achievements.

During his junior and senior years, he became interested in tennis and even won the Boy's State championship. Athletic and disciplined, he played to win, but often had a

difficult time exhibiting good sportsmanship on the court
when he lost a match.

Jerry spent his summers as a lifeguard at the beach,
working at the same job every year from the time he was
fifteen. His duties included swim- and dive-instruction, as
well as supervising the facility. It was a position that the
trim, athletic young man enjoyed, and one that he would
return to every summer until he enlisted in the United States
Marine Corps in 1965.

Yet, in spite of his popularity and his ability to get dates,
some of Jerry's friends believe that he may have suffered
taunts—real or imagined—because of his size. The psychological scars that accompany teen years spent as one of
the smallest boys in the class were deeply rooted in his
psyche. Being—or becoming—a "big guy" may have influenced his tragic fate.

After all, it must have been hard when his younger
brother T, who was two years his junior, became a member
of the football team that Jerry was cheering from the sidelines of the Walton Wright Stadium. T's rugged good looks
and participation on the team earned him notice, but high
school pals of Jerry recall that the younger Akers boy
seemed to lack the intellectual genius that came so naturally
to his older brother.

As youngsters, friends say that Jerry and T shared a
room. But their relationship grew strained over time, with
Jerry jealous of his brother's greater stature, and T struggling to keep pace with Jerry's continual accomplishments.
While Jerry was more charismatic than his younger sibling,
he was also more intense, and confrontational.

T was both handsome and well built. With neatly
clipped, sandy brown hair and powder-blue eyes, he stood
several inches taller than Jerry. By puberty, it was clear
that he had inherited the same indistinguishably deep voice

that had become his older brother's trademark. And T was aware that his broad, muscular shoulders filled out the Sheffield High School football jersey better that his older brother ever could.

T's classmates at the gleaming white educational institution liked to joke that his voice was so low that his utterances entered the room before he did. His easy-going nature and football-player stature won him wild popularity with his peers, yet he seemed to be forever faced with the challenge of living up to his brother's glowing reputation.

While T belonged to the basketball team and the dramatics club, and served as Class Representative for one year, his own personal triumphs seemed to pale in comparison to Jerry's.

The shadow of expectation that seemed to engulf T did not extend to his baby sister Carolyn. Attractive, smart, and extremely well liked, she was counted among the most popular students at Sheffield High. She was voted homecoming queen of her senior class, and was considered by her peers to be the prettiest girl in the entire school. The slender, blonde-haired beauty went on to marry, right out of high school, a young man named Ron Phillips whose family owned a successful business in Nashville, Tennessee.

Ron's prominent employment and respectable salary afforded the couple an opulent home just outside of Sheffield, along the banks of the Tennessee River that continued to be the envy of the Akers family's classmates at Sheffield High.

Growing up, Jerry's increasingly rigid personality and unbending views irritated his siblings. T and Chicken found their older brother inflexible and opinionated and noticed that he sometimes got himself into situations that seemed easily avoidable. While they loved him immensely, the two were also frightened by the way Jerry reacted to the increasingly scary and, in their opinions, unnecessary predicaments in which he often found himself.

Their friends theorized that to compensate for his small stature, Jerry tended to take dangerous risks, often refusing to back down in confrontations with guys who were twice his size. Determined to fight his point, he exhibited a boldness that seemed unwise and daringly risky. T and Carolyn worried that their brother was trying to prove himself too much, like the time in his late teens when he embarked on an exercise regimen so rigorous that it seemed he was destined to kill himself.

For Jerry, doing beyond-the-pale pushups and sit-ups and running countless miles every day were his answer to the teasing stares he routinely received—or imagined—from his peers.

By the end of his senior year, Jerry counted the position of Head Cheerleader among his many accomplishments. His classmates considered him a born leader, and honored him with the "Best All-Round" award. He and fellow cheerleader Brenda Phillips were even voted the "cutest students" at Sheffield High. Jerry and the perky blonde, with her wavy hair and wide, toothy grin, were also elected "Senior Favorites" of the Class of 1960. For Jerry, these designations were yet more impressive titles to add to his lengthy list of credentials.

The distinctions were all part of a banner send-off for the local teen who would join sixty of his classmates at Florence State Teachers College across the river as incoming freshmen. In later years, the school would be renamed the University of Northern Alabama.

CHAPTER FIVE

IN THE FALL OF 1960, JERRY AND HIS BEST FRIEND RAY Walker began their freshman studies at Florence State Teachers College, a local, four-year college located across the O'Neal Bridge in neighboring Florence. Like many of his friends' families, Jerry's parents did not have the resources to buy their young son a car, but the lack of wheels was not a problem. Jerry, Ray, and three other guys from their high school class arranged to catch a ride with a fellow Sheffield High School pal who had his own transportation, agreeing to pay their friend one dollar a week each to drive them to and from the Florence campus.

While being enrolled in the college was exciting for Jerry and Ray, they had already agreed that they would only stay at the campus for two years. Money was tight, and they appreciated the hardship that four years of tuition would heap on their parents. They were certain that if they saved the money they earned at their summer jobs, and took just a little help from their families, they could pull off their dream to transfer to the University of Alabama in their junior year, and to pledge the fraternity Sigma Chi together.

Both men studied hard, with Jerry displaying his usual brilliance and ending his second year with almost perfect grades. He had earned an "A" in every subject, and was expecting to see a 4.0 average on his grade sheet. But the studious perfectionist had become enraged when he opened his report card to find a "B" in ROTC—the Reserved Officers' Training Corps—that pulled down his otherwise perfect score. In his usual confrontational manner, Jerry stormed into the school's ROTC classroom, creating a scene with his professor that nearly ended in a fistfight.

But he was unable to sway the teacher to adjust the grade, and this was incomprehensible to Jerry. In his entire life, he had prided himself at being able to realize his goals—even adding the extra inches he longed for to his height. But now, for the first time, he was faced with the reality that he could do nothing to change his professor's mind. His "B" would stand, and Jerry could barely tolerate not getting what he wanted. Nevertheless, he managed to control himself.

In the fall of 1962, Jerry and Ray left their insular, small-town world and the equally small-time college they had commuted to for two years to transfer to the more prestigious University of Alabama.

The sprawling campus was a three-hour car ride from Sheffield, in the city of Tuscaloosa, which had once been the state's capital until President Thomas Jefferson ordained it changed to Birmingham.

When Jerry arrived at the lovely landscaped campus, with its imperial, wide-trunk trees, and red-brick Jeffersonian-style architecture, the city had fewer than 70,000 residents and was considered to be the fifth largest in Alabama. Union troops during the Civil War had burned all but four of the University's original fourteen buildings, leaving intact only the gracious President's Mansion, the lovely Gorgas House, the Roundhouse, and the Observatory, all now prominent symbols of the campus. The history of the school inspired Jerry and Ray to aspire to something larger than their own provincial beginnings.

But while he and Ray found that the students had access to a small strip of bars and eateries that lined the city streets, they quickly realized that much more exciting activities took place on the grassy campus.

For Jerry and Ray, both twenty years old, the experience of living away from home, and far from the protective environments of their families and friends, was both illuminating and humbling. Now they were but two ordinary guys in a community of eight thousand students. Jerry didn't share a dormitory room with Ray, and instead moved to a small apartment just off campus sometime before the second semester of his junior year.

But the two young men did everything together, including rushing Sigma Chi, the fraternity they had chosen while they were still students at Sheffield High. Although Jerry had been offered an opportunity to rush Kappa Alpha, he stayed true to his pledge to his friend and opted for admission to the mutually agreed-upon fraternity. For Jerry, belonging to the popular brotherhood was very important, a sign of acceptance into the larger society. It was his hope that both he and Ray would be granted membership in the fraternity that has a chapter at almost every large public and private institution in the United States, as well as abroad.

Members of Sigma Chi were surprised when Jerry didn't heed their advice to enroll in classes that were easiest and would afford him the grades necessary to qualify for the fraternity. They informed Ray that they were worried that his pal had put himself at risk by signing up for too many difficult classes during the time that he was rushing the fraternity, itself a formidable task. They did not know Jerry's track record, or that he was never one to take the easy road to success. He enjoyed presenting himself with challenges, and derived great satisfaction from coming out a winner at his own game.

Ray knew that it would have been out of character for

Jerry to reduce his course load and sign up for classes that he didn't find challenging and formidable. He was not the least bit surprised by his friend's choice to do it the hard way. Ray knew that Jerry would never sit on the sidelines and observe others as they participated in desirable activities, and that he would always be right there in the thick of the action, whether it was as cheerleader of his high school's football team, or as a member of the student council.

Ray also knew that his friend had a natural ability for learning, and was able to study in places that he and other students would find most awkward. While standing on line at a dinner buffet, he could not help but notice that while he and the other guys waiting were busy flirting with the coeds, Jerry was reading his school books, preparing for his upcoming tests.

In spite of the doomsday warnings, both Jerry and Ray were granted entrance into the popular Greek-letter society.

Founded in 1855, Sigma Chi is a Christian-based organization. Founded at Miami University by seven young men who broke off from Delta Kappa Epsilon and formed their own organization, the fraternity's emblem is the white Cross, and membership is granted only to those who can meet its seven exacting criteria—the most important is being a man of good character. For Jerry, acceptance to the fraternity was yet another achievement to add to his growing list of overcoming-the-odds accomplishments.

Members of Sigma Chi remember their frat brother as athletic and highly energetic. They say that Jerry was very involved in the numerous and demanding roles of the fraternity, as well as in other activities at the college. When he first arrived at the school, he immediately tried out for membership on the famed cheerleading squad, and his audition won him status as an alternate. But being a cheerleader-in-waiting was irritating to him. After all, he reasoned, he had already attained so many of his highest and most cherished goals, standing at the window looking in at the other kids eating candy was not acceptable.

It did not take long before Lady Luck, his frequent companion, intervened. A vacancy on the twelve-person junior varsity squad—six men and six women—placed Jerry at the center of the action, donning the school's red-and-white uniform at all of his alma mater's games. The fact that the squad had to attend practice sessions five days a week and participate in all of the mandatory overtime workouts the coach demanded was not at all daunting to Jerry, who appreciated the importance of his position perhaps more than the other members of the cheerleading unit.

The school's weekend football matches were considered the most popular events at the Southern campus. Beginning in the late 1920s, the University of Alabama was most recognized for its winning football team, The Crimson Tide, and revered for its legendary coach, Paul "Bear" Bryant, as well as its famed "Million Dollar Band."

To locals, as well as to national media sports fans, "Bama" football games were never-to-be-missed events. Jerry took great pride as one of the school's most dazzling cheerleaders, chanting victory songs on the sidelines and showcasing contortionistic gymnastic feats during half-time activities. To the sounds of the Million Dollar Band, he and the other cheerleaders showcased their agility and talents, and then took to the bench to watch Colonel Carleton K. Butler direct the marching formations, which included not only the score of the game, but also the exact time on the clock, and the temperature outside.

In his senior year, Jerry rented an apartment off campus with his pal Ray. The accommodations they could afford were sparse and humble, but the two young men congratulated themselves for arriving at senior status. They spent a lot of their senior year enjoying frat parties at the Sigma Chi house on Friday and Saturday nights, and never missed an opportunity to take part in the other parties and social events on campus, though they rarely visited the handful of pubs and bars in downtown Tuscaloosa.

It was during the early part of their senior year that Ray finally witnessed his best friend in a serious relationship. Jerry had become infatuated with—actually in love with—a pretty young woman from Florence. But the romance fizzled shortly after Jerry began his first semester at law school, and he confided in Ray that their breakup had left him heartbroken and distraught. Ray was left to wonder if Jerry would ever be able to love another woman in the same way again.

During the years that Jerry and Ray attended the University of Alabama, the United States was undergoing cataclysmic changes, not only in the Southern states, but throughout the country. Men like Jerry and Ray were part of a vast network of good-ole Southern boys, raised for generations with deeply held and passionate beliefs that black people were intrinsically inferior to white people. Jerry stood with his mouth agape, furious and uncomprehending, as the first black students were enrolled at "his" college. He didn't exactly know what to make of the sea change in society, and he didn't really like it.

In fact, Jerry's graduation preceded, by just one year, that of Vivian Malone the first black student to earn a diploma at his state-funded university. Having grown up in a segregated city, both Jerry and Ray had limited exposure to black people, and Ray noticed that his friend seemed to harbor a particularly malevolent attitude toward the presence of blacks on the campus, although he tried to camouflage his feelings to accommodate prevailing sentiments.

As the second semester of their senior year neared, Jerry learned that his best friend would not be returning to the tiny apartment they had rented together in downtown Tuscaloosa. Ray had enlisted in the Marine Corps, and was going off to Officer Candidate School right after the Christmas holiday. Jerry knew that Ray's father had served in the Corps and, with the conflict in Vietnam quietly escalating, he listened as his friend explained that serving his country was something he felt he had to do.

Jerry respected Ray's decision, and even considered it noble. As he accompanied Ray to the curb of his house on Nineteenth Street to bid him farewell, Jerry momentarily contemplated the idea of enlisting along with him. Jerry's dad, a stern and austere man, had also been a Marine, and had proudly served his country during World War II.

Ray had never had much contact with Jerry's father, William Akers, over the years. He had been to the Akers home countless times over the course of his ten-year friendship with Jerry, and had spent hours with Jerry's mom, Gladys, both in church and as a Boy Scout under her direction. But his contact with Jerry's dad had been limited to a nod and a handshake upon entering and leaving the family's cozy brick house. So he was surprised when the senior Akers came running out of the house after him as he was getting ready to climb into his car. The gangly young man remained silent as Jerry's father placed his hand on his shoulder and said, "Remember son, a dead Marine is soon a forgotten hero."

The three men awkwardly saluted a goodbye. It would not be until two years later that Ray and Jerry would embrace in a chance encounter in the jungles of Vietnam.

In May of 1964, Jerry graduated from the University of Alabama with a Bachelor of Arts in Political Science and a letter of acceptance to the University of Virginia, School of Law. From the moment he arrived at the prestigious law school in September, Jerry moved to redefine himself. The young man, who had gone through the last twenty-one years of his life as Jerry Ray, would register simply as Jeremy Akers, dropping the Southern-sounding double name of his childhood. He successfully completed his first year of studies at the highly regarded law school. While he maintained excellent grades and seemed able to put his failed relationship with the young woman from Florence behind him, he did not return to Charlottesville in the fall.

With the war escalating in Vietnam, and his friend Ray now stationed in Southeast Asia, he felt it his duty to serve his country. He had been raised in a family where patriotism and loyalty were exalted above all else. His father had served in the Marine Corps in World War II and saw combat overseas. In the fall of 1965, Jerry enlisted in the United States Marine Corps in Birmingham, Alabama, and applied for one of its programs to receive a commission. It seemed unusual for a young man who had been a cheerleader to choose the most rigorous, demanding branch of the military, but Jerry had learned early how to juggle his varying interests.

His military records note that his job prior to enlisting was listed as "lifeguard" with seven years of experience. His duties were described simply as "guarding lives, swimming and diving instruction, and supervision of premises."

For the United States Marines, involvement in what would turn out to be the nation's longest war had begun on August 2, 1954, eleven years before Jerry Akers entered the service. The arrival of Lieutenant Colonel Victor J. Croizat as a liaison officer with the newly established United States Military Assistance and Advisory Group to the Republic of Vietnam marked the beginning of America's commitment to South Vietnam. But it was not until the spring of 1962 that the United States deployed a Marine Medium Squadron to South Vietnam to provide combat service support to the South Vietnamese Army.

Like all Americans, Jeremy felt angered when news of the Gulf of Tonkin incident hit the papers in August of 1964. The alleged attack on a U.S. aircraft carrier in the waters off the eastern coast of North Vietnam left him and many of his countrymen enraged. The incident triggered an escalation of U.S. involvement in the Republic of Vietnam, and occurred just days before Jeremy began his first semester at the University of Virginia. As was his nature, Jeremy studied diligently, all the time keeping one eye on the events unfolding in Vietnam. He was aware that by the end of his first year of law school, the United States had mobilized more than 40,000 troops in South Vietnam, and word that more men were being called to duty prompted him to put his studies on hold and join the fight. To Jeremy, serving one's country was the noblest thing a man could do, and he had zero tolerance for those who didn't feel the same way.

Jeremy was aware that admission to Officer Candidate School was limited, and reserved only for those who could meet the Marine Corps' demanding criteria. In Birmingham, he was asked to prove himself worthy of entrance by consenting to a rigorous fitness test, as well as a test of his academic aptitude. By all accounts, he had been preparing for this examination since his early teens, beginning with his rigid body-building regimen, and maintenance of his impeccable grades throughout his academic career.

Jeremy, who returned to using the name Jerry during his time in the Marines, was selected for Officer Candidate School (OCS), and as a Private First Class, on December 2, 1965, at the age of twenty-three, he reported for his first day at what members of the Corps refer to as "boot camp for officers."

From the moment he signed on with the Command, he learned what would be expected of a Marine. Upon enlisting in Birmingham, recruiters advised him to show up for his first day of OCS in top physical condition and gave him a handout to take home that was designed to prepare him for what he would encounter during his ten weeks at OCS. The booklet reviewed the importance of physical endurance, especially upper body strength and stamina, and explained that he would be tasked with such rigorous drills as rope climbing, obstacle courses, and individual and group runs of varying lengths, conditioning hikes and stamina-oriented courses. The leaflet also explained that male candidates would be expected to run three miles in less than twenty-eight minutes, and do a minimum of fifty sit-ups in under two minutes.

While the polite, energetic boy from Sheffield, Alabama had always maintained good physical health, including his stint as a lifeguard, none of his prior athletic undertakings had prepared him for the rigorous training he was about to brave.

Dressed in what the Marine Corps insists is "appropriate civilian attire"—a collared shirt, impeccably pressed slacks, and belt—Jerry Akers reported to the six-thousand-acre campus of the United States Marine Corps at Quantico, Virginia, for his first day of Officer Candidate School. With its nineteen buildings, and twenty-five miles of trails, it was considered one of the top military training facilities in the world.

When he enlisted in Birmingham, Jerry had been advised that the school's mission was "to train, evaluate, and screen officer candidates to ensure that they possess the moral, intellectual, and physical qualities for commissioning and the leadership potential to serve successfully as company grade officers in the Fleet Marine Force." But it was not until he began his training that he fully understood the meaning of those words.

With temperatures hovering around the thirty-degree mark, the slender, five-foot, seven-inch Alabama native clutched the small sack of necessities that he had been ordered to bring with him, and made his way across the parking lot to the area marked for check-in. From the minute he announced his name to the Marine in charge of the administrative process, he was indoctrinated into the service. Right from the start, he learned that there were only two ways of doing things, the wrong way, and the Marine way.

As a member of the 40th Officer Candidate Class, he would sign a contract upon completion of the ten-week course of study that obligated him to the Marine Corps for three full years. With his cap yanked tightly over his eyes, hiding the regulation crew cut he had just received, his well-toned muscles concealed beneath a newly assigned uniform, Jerry followed his fellow candidates as they fell into formation on the sprawling lawn outside the school's red-brick barracks. That moment marked the beginning of seventy days of shouting, slapping, shoving, and kicking, and of physical training so rigorous it reduced grown men to tears.

Even before he enlisted in the Corps, Jerry was aware that the Marines was like no other branch of the service, and he was now finding out that Officer Candidate School was like no other training program in the military. Right from the start, his Commanding Officers made it clear that the mission they were undertaking—training their candidates to be Marine officers—was the most demanding mission of the Corps. And it was for that reason that he would endure at OCS a training program that was more challenging than any other in the military services. Its approach was fundamentally different from that of Recruit Training where the objective is to train candidates to obey, react, and follow under the stress of combat. While Recruit Training at Paris Island and San Diego was reputed to be the most physically demanding program of its kind, OCS had the added psychological dimension, making it mentally taxing on Officer Candidate hopefuls.

The goal of OCS, Jerry was about to discover, was to turn out a lieutenant who exhibited the potential to think and to lead under the stress of combat. For Jerry, that difference translated into a basic indoctrination so rigorous that it was designed to "wash out" those individuals not physically or mentally capable of handling extreme amounts of pressure. Historically, the program had a fairly decent "wash out" rate. But Jerry was about to discover that with the Vietnam War escalating overseas, and the intention of the training now focused on readying officer candidates for actual combat, the already challenging program had been stepped up to an even more intense pace.

One of the first lessons he learned was that he'd better make sure that he was always "squared away," the Marine term for *neat*. To his commanding officers, that meant trousers without creases, shoes that are polished, ties that are not too long and with a knot that is neat, belts that are clipped, brass that is shined, hair that is closely cropped. Sideburns and body odor would not be tolerated. According to the Marine way of thinking, neatness is a sign of order and discipline, while sloppiness is a sign of laziness, and there is no tolerance for a lazy officer in the Corps.

The next lesson on the agenda was punctuality. It didn't take long for Jerry to understand that when Reveille sounded at 5:00 a.m., he had exactly thirty minutes—and not a second more—to get dressed, make his rack (the Marine term for *bed*), brush his teeth, shave, and clean his squad bay (the Marine term for *sleeping quarters*). And there were no exceptions. He quickly learned that no matter how late he returned from combat-training exercises the night before, or how badly his body hurt, he'd better be up, neat, and ready to go when the Commander stepped into his squad bay the following morning. Jerry slept alongside his fellow officer candidates in a sprawling barracks lined with two rows of bunk beds and a common latrine. He was to report to breakfast promptly at 5:30 a.m., and had little time to gobble down his morning meal before setting out for a day of training so vigorous it made his bones ache.

Jerry's indoctrination included extreme amounts of physical training, coupled with comprehensive classroom instruction. By the end of the ten weeks, he would be well on his way to becoming a trained leader, ready to direct his men in combat, and not afraid to risk his life for the good of his country. He endured grueling hours learning about basic first aid and weapons systems, and suffered through unending quizzes on the history of the Marine Corps. The idea, he was repeatedly told, was to establish for the officer candidate a basic background in the military way of life, and to provide an understanding of how the military integrates its different tactical strategies. Jerry would learn how to dress and how to march like a Marine.

From early morning until well into the wee hours of the night, his endurance was put to the test, with classes in camouflage, cover and concealment, night combat, and movement courses that consisted of eight different techniques for negotiating obstacles in the field. He learned about the chain of command, about the synchronization between the different branches of service, and about weapons, marksmanship, and the ideology of different weapons systems. And while a good deal of his youth had been spent around guns, his training was now geared toward the use of these weapons in face-to-face combat. He spent hours crawling through mud, climbing up ropes, and hiking until he thought he would drop. There were countless marathon runs, and forced marches in which officer candidates were tasked with carrying gear that weighed in excess of forty pounds for miles. His physical courage, will power, and determination were tested on a daily basis, and in the end, he emerged victorious. On April 1, 1966, he was indoctrinated into the Marines and commissioned Second Lieutenant; a proud moment for the young man from Sheffield, Alabama, whose perfect marksmanship had earned him a weapons score of "A."

Nearly two months later, on May 26, 1966, Jerry Akers completed Officer Candidate School at Quantico. By his side was Ron G. Brown, the friend he had made during his ten weeks of training. The men celebrated their admission into the United States Marine Corps with a day-long graduation ceremony that began with a parade in which all the candidates marched in their camouflage utility greens to the beat of a military band. The highlight of the day was a formal afternoon ceremony attended by friends and family members to which the newly commissioned Marine officers wore for the first time the dressy Service Alpha uniform of a green wool jacket and slacks.

Two days later, on May 28, Jerry began The Basic School (TBS) at Quantico where he continued his indoctrination for another twenty-one weeks. This time, he was greeted with the respect due a Marine Corps officer. Instead of waking before sunrise and training until well after dark, Jerry and the other officers of TBS enjoyed a less strenuous schedule, rising at 7 a.m. and training through 5 p.m. Their accommodations were less spartan. They moved out of their barracks and into officers' quarters in which four men shared a room and had a semi-private lavatory. Their course of instruction also changed from basic Marine indoctrination to learning about combat tactics.

His training now focused specifically on his grade of command, which, he learned, would be the platoon commander's level. He was being schooled on how to be a leader, and his training was aimed at preparing him and his fellow Marines to direct a company of thirty to forty men into combat. He learned specific tactical strategies, and spent time in the field, honing and practicing the skills he was learning. Life as a Marine officer was a perfect fit for Jerry Akers. He thrived on military life and its principles and on his successful development into a man with a title. His self-image had changed and he felt less wary, more confident. He believed in the military and the opportunity for a stronger voice in the community. As the course moved into its final weeks, he grew increasingly aware that his opportunity to serve his country in the war escalating in Southeast Asia was only days away.

October 26, 1966, marked the end of Second Lt. Jerry Akers' formal school training. He was now a Basic Infantry Officer, his bill of description, platoon leader. With his new military rank, Jerry traveled home to Sheffield one last time to spend the holidays with his family before returning to headquarters to receive his orders. In January of 1967, at the age of twenty-four, a bolder, more self-assured Jerry Akers reported to the Fleet Marine Force to receive his assignment. His thirty-one weeks of training had bolstered his ego, and elevated him to a level of self-assurance that he never believed possible.

Akers was flown to the Marine Air Base in St. Louis, Missouri, where he boarded a plane for Vietnam. For the next seven months, he would be a platoon leader, attached to Company L, Third Battalion, Fourth Marines, Third Marine Division. Jerry was proud to wear the Marine uniform and to be a member of the illustrious and colorful Fourth Marines.

On January 12, 1967, Second Lieutenant Jerry Ray Akers arrived in Southeast Asia. Like hundreds of other Marines, he was flown into Da Nang aboard a commercial jet. Trans World Airlines was landing 707s there every six to eight hours, the aircraft filled to capacity with Marine replacements.

Raw Marines like Dennis "Dawg" Thun, who would later join Lima Company and fight alongside Lt. Jerry Akers' platoon, were astonished when they descended the steps of the commercial jet and viewed a base much like Camp Pendleton, the one he had just left behind in California. From television and newspapers they had read, "Dawg" and the others half-expected to face enemy gunfire the second they opened the plane's doors.

The base at Da Nang was not at all the dank jungle that Dawg had anticipated. In fact, it was the size of a small town, and, in addition to the airstrip that was big enough to accommodate military aircraft, it included countless metal Quonset huts, supply depots, movie theaters, and clubs for commissioned and non-commissioned officers. New arrivals spent their first day on the base and received their orders the next morning. Dawg, a Marine grunt fresh from boot camp, swallowed hard when he was given orders to be on the airfield at 1400 hours to board a flight to join his battalion in Dong Ha, just five miles from the Demilitarized Zone—and some of the most intense fighting in Vietnam. Dawg knew from talk around the base that being that far north placed him in extreme danger.

The following morning, when he went out to meet the C130 that would take him to his detail in the North, he was hit with a reality so frightening that he felt a shiver throughout his entire being. The young Marine from Chicago watched as military personnel unloaded fifty body bags containing the latest casualties and placed them onto the tarmac.

With the scene etched in his memory, the trained mortar man boarded the prop plane, and to the roar of its four engines, fastened his seatbelt for the short flight up the coast. He watched from the window as the aircraft touched down at Dong Ha. Leaving the plane, he observed that the rear base for the Third Marine Division was nothing like the one he had just left to the south. There were no Quonset huts, just tents for the men, and military transports and helicopters that ferried the Marines into and out of the base around the clock.

Dawg and the other replacements were directed to an area where they would draw their gear. As he eyed the heaps of equipment, he observed that the canteens and flak jackets had all been used before, and many were riddled with bullet holes and stained with blood. Poking through the piles, he rummaged about until he found two canteens and a flak jacket that looked in decent enough shape to wear. He drew two magazines for his rifle, but making his way back to the staging area, a chilling thought invaded his mind: "I'm not going to a good place."

Jerry Akers was already in Dong Ha when Dawg landed there. But it would be several months before the men's paths would cross and they would be involved in a vicious attack by the enemy that would give Dawg a glimpse of just how intense Jeremy's reaction could be when he believed he had been crossed. After collecting his gear, Dawg and the other Marine replacements boarded a military transport truck and headed inland to Camp Carroll.

The trip took the men west from a relatively flat coastal

area of sand dunes, hedgerows, and scrub brush into a mountainous jungle. The Marine artillery base at Cam Lo had been named for Captain James J. Carroll, who was killed by friendly fire during the October 5, 1966, assault on Hill 484. Army bulldozers had been used to level the terrain and clear some ground for heavy artillery equipment. Dawg observed battle-hardened Marines, many of them with jungle rot, a fungus that causes uncontrollable itching, as the truck braked to a stop at the camp.

Jerry, who had arrived "in country" several weeks before, would later be called to defend the base.

CHAPTER SIX

As A PLATOON LEADER AT DONG HA, JERRY WAS IN COM-
mand of three squads, each one comprised of twelve
Marines. He and the leaders of the three other platoons that
made up Lima Company would follow the orders of the
Company Commander. Located on the coast of the China
Sea, Dong Ha was the rear base for the Third Marine Division. The small, muddy Marine camp in the northern part
of South Vietnam had a short, 800-foot landing strip, and
was located just south of the Demilitarized Zone (DMZ).
It was the middle of monsoon season when Jerry landed in
Vietnam.

As a second lieutenant, he shared a 10 by 20–foot tent
with fellow officers—three platoon leaders and three platoon sergeants—and slept in a sleeping bag on an Army
cot that was draped with mosquito netting. In the field, he
dozed on the ground alongside his men, often in holes they
had dug for themselves. Their light-weight jungle uniforms
provided little protection from the torrential downpours and
cold, moonless nights.

Jerry and members of his platoon spent only a few days
at the base camp before they were ordered into combat on
January 16, 1967, as part of Operation Prairie, a search-
and-clear mission that was underway in the Quang Tri
Province. The maneuver ended on January 31, 1967, and
Jerry and his platoon were immediately reassigned to Operation Prairie II.

Three weeks later, Akers was leading his men on a search-and-clear mission through the brush northwest of Cam Lo, in the Quang Tri Province, when a North Vietnamese Army (NVA) battalion launched a fierce predawn attack with mortars, hand grenades, and automatic weapons. Jerry and his platoon came under intense fire from the NVA but the second lieutenant held his ground. Braving the vicious assault, he organized his men and directed such blistering fire on the advancing enemy that they were forced to break contact and withdraw. Later that day, the enemy attacked again, and Jerry's platoon sergeant and corpsman were both wounded by enemy fire. Jerry, too, was hit in the leg. Seeing that his men were hurt and in exposed positions, Jerry advanced through enemy fire, carried them to safety, and administered first aid. As the firefight continued, Jerry encouraged his men and assisted the wounded. He refused to be evacuated, and stayed with his unit for two days until reinforcements finally arrived. He exhibited such bravery that he was awarded the Marines' third highest honor, the Silver Star for Valor.

After receiving treatment for his injury, Jerry returned to the base at Dong Ha. One afternoon, when he got back to his tent, he was introduced to a new roommate, Tom Downes. The first lieutenant had been in Vietnam for almost a year, and was nearing the end of his tour when he was transferred to Lima Company and assigned to act as executive officer of the Company and its four platoon leaders. The two quickly became friends, but Jerry never let on that he had just recently received the Silver Star. Tom only heard about it through others in the camp.

Jerry and his platoon participated in Operation Prairie III between March 19 and April 5, according to his military service record. Meanwhile back in the States, the anti-war movement was building. On April 15, a massive demonstration was held throughout the country against United States involvement in Vietnam. New York newspapers featured photographs of protestors burning draft cards in Central Park, and similar rallies were headlined throughout the nation.

As demonstrators marched at home, Jerry and his new roommate, Tom Downes, fought side by side against the Viet Cong before their Battalion was rotated back to Okinawa to reorganize, get new equipment, and bring the unit up to its normal complement of men. They sailed together through Subic Bay in the Philippines and stopped at the port-of-call for five hours before continuing on to Okinawa. Tom knew Subic Bay well, having spent several years there during his youth while his father was in the Navy. His friend was in the mood for a cocktail, but drinking was forbidden on board the ship. The two men hopped aboard a launch for the short run to the dock. Once ashore, they headed for the Subic Bay Officers Club, which was set on the waterfront and surrounded by lofty palms. As they approached the entrance to the sprawling white compound with the red tile roof, they learned that a party was going on inside, and a brawny officer guarding the door gave them the brush-off. Looking past him, they could see that all of the naval officers—many accompanied by their wives—were wearing their dress whites.

While First Lt. Downes and Second Lt. Akers were clean-shaven and neat, they realized that the utility green uniforms and heavy jungle boots they were wearing were not exactly appropriate for the festivities going on just a few feet away from where they stood. Refusing to let them in, the heavy-set naval officer blocked the club's doorway, but his efforts to bar the men's entrance was met with resistance by Jerry, who moved within a few inches of the stocky man and demanded that he and his officer friend be granted admittance. It was clear to Tom that Jerry was not interested in compromise, even though the man he was confronting was considerably bigger than him. Jerry wanted to fight the guy, and seemed unwilling to listen to reason. His behavior did not surprise Tom. On the contrary, he knew that his friend had a temper and would never back down, no matter what the odds.

Sensing that his subordinate was ready to attack, and not wanting to offend the officers inside, Lt. Downes stepped between the two, and asked the naval officer if there was another club nearby. Suddenly, the three men were joined by a full Navy Commander who directed them to Cubi's Point. Facing the superior officer, Jerry backed down. The two men hailed a cab for the Cubi's Point Officers Club that was located on the grounds of the Naval Air Station. But once inside, they were disappointed to find the bar practically empty, so they stayed just long enough to have a couple of drinks.

Jerry's drawn-out confrontation with the officer at the first club had eaten up much of their shore time, and suddenly it became evident to Tom that they were dangerously close to missing their ship's scheduled departure for Okinawa. At Tom's insistence, the two Marines departed the club, flagged down a taxi, and headed back to Fleet Landing, where the launches were docked. When they arrived, they discovered that the last boat had already left for the ship and they were at risk of being left behind—and potentially facing a court martial. As Tom worried about his future in the Marines, Jerry took action, leaping aboard a twenty-six-foot launch and convincing the helmsman to shuttle them out to their vessel before it left port. Realizing that he did not have much of a choice, Tom joined his friend, who was not the least bit concerned about their predicament. As they neared the ship, Tom could see that the seamen aboard were in the midst of raising the launches and gangplank. With just seconds to spare, the two reached the boat, jumped onto the ramp, and Tom breathed a sigh of relief.

In Okinawa, Tom found himself in the role of peacemaker on more than one occasion. The young Marine officer remembered one incident in which he and Jerry had gone to a club with two other officers and become embroiled in a confrontation with officers from the Reunicin Armed Forces Police, who had a reputation for harassing personnel on leave. The four, who were all dressed in civilian clothes, were having drinks together at a table and making some noise. Several members of the military police force approached them, demanding to see some ID. But when the first officer handed over his card, and advised the policeman that they were all military officers, his comment was dismissed out of hand. Instead, the cop demanded to see IDs from all four men seated at the table. Finding their behavior obnoxious and pushy, Jerry stood up, announced he had had enough, and declared that it was time to "clean the floor" with the police, all of whom were armed with billy clubs and side arms. It took more than a little convincing from Tom and the other members of his party before Jerry backed down and agreed to leave the nightclub.

As they walked out, Tom, who hailed from the northeast, thought to himself, "no wonder we had such a hard time winning the Civil War." It was clear to him that his friend was a gentleman of the old school, a man of honor who would not accept or ignore any slight. Jerry was afraid of nothing, and no one.

Jerry returned to the base at Dong Ha, but Tom remained in Okinawa and was sent back to the United States at the end of his tour. Though Tom was happy to be headed home to a wife he hadn't seen in months, there was a piece of him that regretted leaving Vietnam. The young Marine lieutenant felt that the long and arduous year he had spent "in country" truly had a purpose, and that the role he played was an important one, one on which he placed a high value. He was certain that Jerry—who he knew did not have a wife or even a special girl to go home to—felt the same way.

But Tom could not have anticipated how his countrymen would react when he flew back to the West Coast. Stepping off the plane in his Marine uniform, the lieutenant was stunned when people in the terminal began spitting at him, and accusing him of being a killer. Racing to the men's room, he quickly pulled off the uniform he had been so proud to wear and changed into street clothes to escape the taunts.

He had been home only a couple of weeks when he received a letter from Jerry describing how a surprise attack with mortars had killed dozens of Marines at Dong Ha. The territory was considered a "safe area" and therefore none of the men had dug any holes to protect themselves from enemy attack, a mistake that turned out to be fatal. Jerry had been hurt in the fighting, but his injury was not serious and he was able to return to duty soon after. Within days, he was back with his platoon and taking part in Operation Prairie IV. The Operation proved a blood-bath for the 26th Marines, with 164 men killed and 999 wounded. But Jerry's platoon was in Operation Prairie for only two days before the men were reassigned to Operation Hickory, the first major Marine thrust into the DMZ.

On May 29, Jerry and his company were taking fire from North Vietnamese troops as they advanced up a hill. Another company was ascending the same hill from the other side as the Viet Cong fired on them from emplacements farther up the hillside.

Dennis Dawg Thun, a member of Lima Company, was there with Second Lieutenant Akers as the Marines moved forward. Throughout his tour of duty, Dawg and members of his mortar unit were routinely called upon to participate in sweeps of hills that had been deemed strategic by their commanding officers. The young Marine spent his entire thirteen-month tour in the jungles of the northern portion of South Vietnam.

It was one of the areas most heavily sprayed with the herbicide Agent Orange, which was applied continuously throughout the time that he and Jerry were on tour there. When he had first arrived "in country," Dawg was assigned to Camp Carroll, where he slept in a tent. But for weeks at a time, he was ordered to participate in night sweeps of the area that had him traipsing through the broad-leaf foliage of the dense, jungle-like terrain. Night after night, he endured the frenetic buzz of mosquitoes swarming about in his helmet, and suffered from a case of jungle rot so severe that layers of his skin flaked off from scratching at the bug bites that covered his body. During the monsoons, he braved nights of pouring rain, sleeping in holes he had dug for himself, and fighting off the mosquitoes, snakes, and leeches that lurked all around him. Often, his clothing was so damp that seventy-degree temperatures had him feeling colder than any winter evening he had ever endured in his hometown of Chicago. Yet, despite the atrocious conditions, he found his nights sweeping the jungle preferable to those he spent at the firebases that were riddled with rats.

Crawling on his hands and knees, Dawg, who had been trained as a mortar man during his six months at Camp Pendleton, was keeping an eye on his superior as he made his way up the hill. In previous battles, he had served under

Jerry Akers as a forward observer. But this time, he was about ten feet behind him. He noted that the Second Lieutenant lay just off to his right, and was facing uphill. Another Marine, no more than ten feet away from Dawg's right shoulder, lay on the ground just behind Akers.

Keeping his head low to avoid the continuous barrage of enemy gunfire, Dawg was astounded when he saw Jerry spring to his feet and point his M16 rifle at the head of the Marine next to him.

"I'm gonna f—king kill you, mother f——r!" Akers screamed at the grunt. "You f—king shot me, you bastard! And I'm gonna f—king take you out!"

Bullets whizzed by from up the hill as Marines lying on the ground nearby watched the unfolding drama in disbelief. Dawg kept firing at enemy positions, while keeping a close eye on the confrontation that was going on just a few feet away. Suddenly it became clear that Akers had been shot in the buttocks, and was convinced that one of his own men—the Marine who lay cowering on the ground with Jerry's rifle aimed at his head—had pulled the trigger. Apparently, seconds after he was shot, Jerry had quickly turned to look behind him. When he noted that he had only friendly troops to his rear, he immediately surmised that he had been targeted by one of his own men.

Jerry had heard stories of platoon leaders killed in action, not by the enemy, but by disgruntled members of their own platoon. But he could not believe it was happening to him. In a rage, he continued to scream threats at the ashen-faced young grunt who lay wide-eyed on the ground with a look of sheer terror emblazoned on his face.

Dawg lay frozen on the ground, worried for the poor guy's safety, when suddenly he spied an enemy soldier pop up from a spider hole in front of him. Instantly, he and the other Marines opened fire on the man and then watched as he dropped to the ground. It was only then that Jerry and the others realized that they had been advancing over enemy soldiers who were dug into the hill.

Akers and his company pulled off the hill that night, and moved back to a safer position where choppers were able to evacuate the dead and wounded, and bring in food and supplies. But the enemy assault continued through the night and some of the Marines were hit and killed by 122-mm rockets. Jerry was flown to safety and hospitalized with gunshot wounds to both buttocks.

It was just weeks before this battle that Jerry had been reunited with his childhood friend, Ray Walker, which had turned out to be a lucky break for Jerry and his parents. He had heard that Ray had been assigned to the base at Dong Ha. But his old pal had no idea that Jerry was an officer there.

As Ray stepped out of one of the buildings on the base, he heard a voice over the loudspeaker beckoning him to another building. Hurrying to get to his destination, he brushed by an officer who immediately challenged him, saying, "Don't you salute lieutenants, Sergeant?" Turning to shoot the lieutenant a dirty look, Ray suddenly realized that the officer was his old friend, Jerry Akers. Jerry had learned that Ray was stationed there and tracked him down to say hello.

The two men enjoyed a great reunion, and caught up on old times. A few weeks later, Ray learned that Jerry's company and battalion had been in a deadly firefight, had sustained numerous casualties, and were being evacuated back to the base by helicopter. Racing to the runway, the lanky, dark-haired Marine scanned the stretchers that lined the airstrip in search of his childhood friend. Finally, he found Jerry, and learned that, although he had been wounded, he was going to be okay. Relieved that his buddy had made it out alive, he returned to the barracks, and sat down to write a letter to Jerry's mother. He wanted to advise Mrs. Akers that her son was in pretty good shape.

Normally, it took three to four days for a letter mailed from Vietnam to reach Sheffield. But in a bizarre twist of fate, Ray's correspondence took just a day and a half to arrive. It reached the Akers home just hours after Marine Corps personnel had visited the family to inform them that Jerry had been wounded in action. But that is all that they were able to tell Jerry's parents. Hours later, Ray's letter arrived and Mr. and Mrs. Akers breathed a sigh of relief.

Jerry did not return to combat until the middle of June. On July 1, the Marine Corps elevated him to the rank of First Lieutenant. His underlings would now salute him. He continued to lead his platoon in a variety of operations until he was made an Aerial Observer in August of 1967. He went on to display the same kind of courage in the air as he did on the ground, and was later awarded an Air Medal. His military service "in country" also earned him the Vietnamese Service Medal with Two Stars.

Jerry went on to receive another Air Medal for his heroism, and was also awarded a Gold Star for his bravery. In addition to his medals and awards, Jerry earned points with his men. While he followed the Marine Corps' strict code of conduct, and never fraternized with a "stripe" (enlisted man), Jerry was well liked by his troops, admired for his keen leadership and his devotion to his men.

In his new role as Aerial Observer assigned to fly on a single-engine plane, he went out of his way to locate members of his own unit who were stationed on the ground for special air drops. One day, Dawg and others in the unit were carrying out orders to perform a sweep of a hill when they observed a small aircraft circling overhead. Suddenly, *Playboy* magazines, packs of cigarettes, and candy bars came raining down on them. Looking up at the plane, the grunts saw their lieutenant waving through the window. The men had no idea that he had been transferred to the Headquarters Battalion of the Third Marines, and that he had received training as a pilot before he enlisted in the service. It was not the last time that Akers would deliver special gifts to his men. Whenever it was possible, he would find his unit in the field and bestow precious commodities like cigarettes on them from above.

On October 14, 1967, First Lieutenant Jerry Ray Akers returned to the United States after his back was seriously injured in a plane crash. When he left Vietnam, among his medals were two Purple Hearts, the Vietnamese Cross of Gallantry with Gold, and the coveted Silver Star. During his tour of duty, he had been wounded five times, and according to a spokesman for the U.S. Marines, he had participated in thirteen major operations. He had also been repeatedly exposed to a dangerous chemical.

An estimated nineteen million gallons of the plant killer Agent Orange was used in South Vietnam during the conflict, with the broadest use of it applied by air from C123's during the height of the war—1967–1968—the time that Jerry Akers was stationed there. It would be several years after the U.S. military left South Vietnam before adverse health effects developed in military personnel as a result of exposure to the herbicide and others that were applied. The earliest health concerns about Agent Orange were about the product's contamination with dioxin. In tests on laboratory animals, dioxin caused a wide variety of diseases, many of them deadly.

Studies performed on those exposed to Agent Orange turned up a variety of disturbing findings. The Vietnam Veteran Outreach Program, which was disbanded in the late 1980s due to lack of funds, published a summary of illnesses suffered by those exposed to high concentrations of the herbicide. Among them are Cloracne, liver dysfunction, cancers, birth defects, and severe personality disorders. Psychiatric symptoms include violence, irritability, anger, severe depression, suicide, frenzied (manic) behavior, tremors, memory loss, loss of concentration, and severe personality changes. It is unclear whether Jerry Akers suffered any ill effects from his repeated exposure.

In January of 1968, Jerry again reported to the Marine Corps Base in Quantico, Virginia, and was assigned to a seven-month stint as an instructor of the Basic Officers Extension Course. In August of 1968, he was elevated to the rank of Captain and became an instructor of the Orientation Course at The Basic School, where he taught infantry squad tactics.

In 1969, he was transferred to the Temporary Disability Retired List. His status as a disabled veteran entitled him to military benefits, which included a small stipend on which he could live.

Later that year, he and his friend Robert Brown, whom he had met in 1966 at Officer Candidate School in Quantico, took off for Europe. For Jerry, it would be a long-overdue vacation, and an opportunity to pal around the continent with one of his closest Marine buddies. Their first stop was Rome, where they rented a car and leisurely drove the Italian countryside en route to Barcelona, Spain. One of the highlights of their lengthy adventure was diving into the cool waters of the Mediterranean from the lofty cliffs of the gorgeous Spanish city on the sea.

Upon returning to the United States, Jerry re-enrolled at the University of Virginia at Charlottesville, where he resumed his studies at its prestigious School of Law. When he returned to the sprawling campus in September of 1969, he decided, once again, to drop his childhood name of

Jerry, and assume his given name of Jeremy R. Akers. He had always dreamed of bettering himself through education, and did little to hide his desire to flee the stigma of his rural roots and join the ranks of the nation's upwardly mobile urban professionals. He was convinced that the more formal name was better suited to the profession he had chosen to pursue.

Because Jeremy was now older than many of his classmates, he opted to forgo dormitory-style living and to seek accommodations off campus. During his second year, he found an ideal arrangement through a friend he had made in the Marine Corps. Ron Castille had been sharing a grand old country house with four other students just outside of Charlottesville. And as luck would have it, a spot opened up when one of the roommates entered the military.

It was a perfect opportunity for Jeremy, not only because he would gain housing, but also because he would be sharing the house with men like himself. Men who had served their country in the United States military. He would now reside in the expansive Georgian-style house with five Marines, including Castille, who had lost a leg in Vietnam, and who would go on to serve as a Supreme Court Justice in the state of Pennsylvania.

Jeremy rarely spoke of his time in the service, and he never once mentioned the Silver Star he was awarded for his bravery. For him, military service was the yardstick by which he measured a person's worthiness as a friend. But it was not something to boast about, even with his fellow officers. Even before his stint in the Marines, he had been a proud patriot. But his loyalty to America, and to his fellow servicemen, intensified after his time in the Corps and his service in Vietnam. He did nothing to hide his disdain for those who had not served, and as the years passed, he grew increasingly intolerant of those with no military background.

Jeremy's circle of friends did not include a single man who had not served his country in the armed forces and seen active duty. His buddies found the former Marine captain very conservative in his thinking, although he did not live the traditional lifestyle that one equates with right-wing thinkers. He was libertarian in his views, and was a loyal friend. Pals like his new housemate Don Boswell, also a Marine, believed that he was someone who could be counted on if there was ever a need.

But his new housemates would soon learn that going out on the town with Jeremy could spell trouble. He had a tendency to get himself involved in fights on a regular basis, and seemed to find it impossible to walk away from potentially explosive situations, even if they put himself and others in harm's way. He was opinionated and brazenly blunt, and his need to tell people what was on his mind created awkward moments, like the time he told one of his roommates that the woman he was dating was unattractive.

Although his outbursts were usually sugar-coated in Southern civility, his friends noticed that his words could be especially harsh after indulging in a few cocktails. While he was not much of a drinker, his cronies knew that when Jeremy had a few glasses of whiskey his blunt comments could be mean and hurtful. Don and his housemates joked that Jeremy's personality was the total opposite of a politician. He never worried what others thought of him, and cared little whether he was liked or hated.

For Don, Jeremy's style could not have been more different from his own. Like Jeremy, he too had been out of school to fulfill his military service in the Marine Corps, and had returned to complete his law studies the year that Jeremy moved into their house. And while Don and Jeremy became good friends, their military service and the fact that they were both enrolled at law school were about the only things the two men had in common.

Don was diligent about his studies, and serious about his education. He attended all of his classes, and set aside ample time to study for his exams. Jeremy, on the other hand, skipped lectures for months at a time. If he thought it was a good ski day, he'd hop in the car and head off to a resort. But he was so bright that he could cram for a week or two and pass his tests without worry.

Even the way that Don and Jeremy approached their leisure activities set them apart, with Don opting to observe and enjoy, and Jeremy preferring a more hands-on approach. On their scuba diving trips to the Bahamas, Don liked to linger under the sea, taking in the wonders of the deep and observing the colorful varieties of tropical fish that swam quietly around him; Jeremy chose a more aggressive style, deriving great pleasure from chasing after the first decent-sized fish that he spotted until he captured and killed it.

Even Jeremy's approach to athletics was contrary, and more intense than Don's or anyone else's in the house that the five men shared. Obsessed with physical fitness, Jeremy routinely embarked on a regimen that included three hundred push-ups, four hundred sit-ups, and a fifteen-mile run. He was totally dedicated to keeping himself in shape, placing his own physical well-being before everything else in his life. So much so that before a final exam, he would wake up unusually early, hit the streets for a fifteen-mile run, and then top off his morning constitutional with one hundred push-ups. Jeremy's intense workouts, coupled with his compact, five-foot, seven-inch frame, prompted Don to nickname his roommate "Little Tarzan."

His well-sculpted physique, and his wild, almost untamable personality made Jeremy popular with women. His dating was somewhat limited by the fact that the law school had just opened its doors to women, and there were little more than a handful of females enrolled at the campus during his time there. Nevertheless, his friends would later describe him as a sort of James Bond type, a man who had countless opportunities to date, but who made little commitment to the women he dated.

As far as Jeremy and his friends were concerned, he was not the marrying kind. His commitment seemed to be to himself first and foremost, and he did not come across as someone who could or would give freely to others. And while he was extremely possessive and solicitous toward his girlfriends, he showed no interest in getting involved in a long-term relationship, and even less interest in the bonds of matrimony.

Yet, friends say, he operated under an archaic honor system that made him jealous and possessive of the women in his life. For instance, the way he reacted upon learning that an old girlfriend had taken up with one of his pals: Unable to let go of their former relationship, Jeremy felt compelled to interrogate his friend, asking pointed questions about every aspect of the relationship, in spite of the fact that it was he who had ended the liaison with the young woman.

Even his commitment to his studies at the University of Virginia did not seem to hold the same importance that they once did. Unlike in the past, when he diligently remained true to his endeavors, he now seemed easily distracted. The promise of a good day of skiing, or a sudden offer to scuba dive in the Bahamas were all it took to lure him away from his classes. Somehow, the excitement of being at the highly-regarded school of law where he had once longed to be matriculated paled in comparison to the life-and-death situations he had experienced as a platoon leader in Viet-

nam. The military stipend that he was receiving from the
Marine Corps for his disability helped him to pay the rent,
and afforded him the chance to travel whenever the opportunity arose, and he took full advantage of any invitations
that came his way.

During one summer break from the University of Virginia, he agreed to work for his favorite cousin, Annette
Clark Dodd, as a clerk at the Birmingham law firm where
she practiced. The job required that he perform a variety
of tasks, everything from writing briefs to pulling files in
court. Jerry had always enjoyed a close relationship with
Annette, whom he considered both brilliant and accomplished. Even though she was eight years his senior, Jerry
counted her among his closest friends. He seemed to feel
comfortable confiding in her, and he often used her as a
sounding board to bounce off his ideas.

He was flattered when she asked him to come to work
for her firm, and happily accepted the invitation. While in
the city, Jeremy decided to contact his old friend from elementary school, Ray Walker. He had heard that Ray had
married and moved to Birmingham with his young bride.
The two men agreed to meet over lunch. Right from the
start, Ray was taken aback by his high school chum's angry
demeanor. He had not seen his old friend since their reunion at the U.S. military base in Dong Ha, Vietnam, yet
it took only minutes for Ray to observe that Jeremy's time
in the military seemed to have changed him. He barely
recognized his old friend, whom he referred to as Jerry. As
they sat talking over sandwiches, Ray saw that the clean-
cut gentleman, who once was elected leader of his class at
Sheffield High School, was gone.

The new Jerry was confrontational, and outraged at the
way his world had changed in the few years that he had
been away. He was critical of the move toward desegre-

gation in the South, and full of enough palpable anger to make his friend afraid of him. During that summer, Ray noticed that Jerry was spending more time than ever partying the nights away. And he learned from a mutual friend that it was Jerry who had been at the center of the ugly fight that had broken out during a bachelor party held that summer.

Jeremy returned to the University of Virginia in the fall, but did not stay for long, opting instead to move to the West Coast to join a friend in the San Francisco Bay area. Friends believe that he was drawn to California's temperate climate and the promise of a good time. He decided to continue his studies at the University of California School of Law, Boalt Hall in Berkeley. Upon completion of several courses, he qualified for his Juris Doctorate from the University of Virginia, and on June 4, 1972, he was awarded his diploma, not long after being admitted to the State Bar of California. Subsequently, he would be admitted to the State Bar of Florida, and the Bar of the Supreme Court of the United States.

In 1973, Jeremy was removed from the Marine Corps' Temporary Disability Retired List, and granted an honorable discharge. His impressive résumé landed him a prestigious position in the nation's capital. At the age of thirty-four, he began a job as staff counsel to the House Select Committee on Assassinations. The committee had been assembled to investigate the death of President John F. Kennedy, and, as counsel, Jeremy formulated and wrote an investigative outline identifying intermediate objectives and ultimate issues to be resolved over a two-year period of investigation.

It was while working on this committee that he met Patricia Duff, who would remain a lifelong friend. The striking socialite with the movie star looks had come to

Washington after her efforts to gain employment overseas failed. When she learned that the House Select Committee on Assassinations was hiring, the lanky, fair-haired beauty turned up at the office dressed to impress and with her résumé in hand.

Attractive, smart, and from a "good" family, Duff was very much Jeremy's type. A graduate of the International School of Brussels at the age of seventeen, Patricia returned to the United States, where she enrolled at Barnard College, sister school to Columbia University, in New York City. Her plan was to study to become a diplomat or a foreign correspondent, but when her parents divorced after her freshman year, she was forced to drop out of the Ivy League school.

After a short stint in Switzerland with a high school boyfriend from Brussels, she returned to the United States and attended Georgetown University, where she majored in international economics. Jeremy's friend Bill Ranger was a student at the campus and would always recount to Jeremy how his heart started pounding every time he saw the breathtaking blonde walking along the cement paths of the Georgian-style campus.

Upon graduation from the predominantly male school, Patricia returned to Europe but had little success finding employment. Discouraged by her fruitless search, she came back to Washington, where she learned of the opening with the newly formed committee. Her new position placed her in constant contact with Jeremy, and the two became fast friends. She was the just the kind of woman that Jeremy found attractive, as he tended to gravitate to women from well-heeled families, even though his own background was much more modest. And while Jeremy and Patricia liked each other, their relationship remained strictly on a platonic level. Patricia found her new companion fun, charming, and

bright. As a member of the research team that Jeremy supervised, she and her colleagues spent much of their time
looking into the activities of the Mob and the CIA.

Jeremy supervised and directed the investigative team of
research assistants and criminal investigators, and coordinated and negotiated policy decisions between the committee, local police departments, the Federal Bureau of
Investigation, and the Central Intelligence Agency. He also
supervised ballistic, fingerprint, handwriting, and soil/fiber
analysis projects, and planned, coordinated, wrote testi-
mony for, and conducted Congressional hearings, including
direct and cross-examination of witnesses in televised sessions.

Even his serious position and the important role that he
was playing in the lengthy investigation did not stop him
from pulling the pranks that set him apart from his colleagues on Capitol Hill. He thought nothing of calling up
a co-worker and pretending to be a Supreme Court justice
phoning to admonish him or her for some infraction. While
some found Jeremy's antics hysterically funny, others were
not amused.

It was during his first year on the job that he was introduced to Nancy Richards, who, at the time, was working
as a researcher for the Senate Foreign Relations Committee.
A mutual friend had suggested he meet the charming brunette, who had previously worked as a speechwriter for the
colorful North Carolina senator, Sam Ervin, before landing
her current research position with the internationally
minded committee.

From their very first date, there seemed to be electricity
in the air. At first, Jeremy was completely taken with the
brainy socialite from one of New York's wealthiest sub-
urbs, Westchester County. He found the curvaceous, five-
foot, four-inch brunette with the ample bosom and

twenty-four-inch waist a knockout. But it wasn't just her looks that captivated Jeremy's interest. Her beauty, sophistication, and worldliness were what really seemed to charm him. That she had been brought up in such a "proper" home, yet could kick up her heels and have a little fun, was intriguing and compelling to him.

Their mutual infatuation was so clearly evident to outsiders that the couple appeared to sparkle whenever they were together. Jeremy found himself attracted to Nancy's vivacious personality and her brilliant mind. In short, she was the type of woman he had always wanted—someone he could not even begin to imagine could ever be capable of disappointing him. He could talk for hours with her about politics, world affairs, and even obscure pieces of literature and never seem to tire. To him, she was smart, spirited, and, most important, a representation of everything he aspired to become. The eloquent, full-figured woman hailed from the kind of background he had only dreamed about. While he had always gravitated to women from well-to-do backgrounds, Nancy's pedigree was particularly impressive. The granddaughter of a wealthy businessman, she had enjoyed a life of privilege that included a boarding-school education, first-class travel, fancy clothes, and the poise that comes from having the "right" upbringing.

CHAPTER SEVEN

NANCY WAS BORN IN NEW YORK CITY ON JANUARY 16, 1951. Her mother, Susan, was twenty-eight years old when she and her first husband took their baby daughter home from the hospital.

A society girl from a wealthy New York family, Nancy's mother had been accustomed to a lifestyle that included Junior League functions and gala society balls. Raised in an exclusive Northeast suburb, she and her sister enjoyed all the privileges afforded to children of high society. The girls' parents showered their daughters with fancy clothes, expensive jewels, and trips around the world.

Shortly after her birth, Nancy was baptized as a Roman Catholic, the religious faith of her father. The adorable little girl with the Shirley Temple curls spent three years being indulged as an only child before the birth of her brother, John on March 13, 1954.

Together, they enjoyed several years as a family, but, unbeknownst to the little girl and her brother the marriage of their parents was disintegrating. Nancy's mother would later confide that she and her father had little in common. Ultimately, they parted ways. Susan asked her husband to relinquish his rights to the children, which he did, and the new divorcee—still uncomfortable in the 1950s about the none-too-popular status—set her sites on finding a suitable new husband from her affluent social circle.

Still in elementary school, Nancy could barely comprehend the news that she would no longer be seeing her father. But when she tried to talk to her mother about him, she was admonished *never* to mention his name again. Nancy would later tell friends that she had spent many nights in the privacy of her curtain-laced bedroom, crying herself to sleep, mourning the loss of her beloved daddy. But her tears did nothing to bring back the dark-haired man who had willingly bid his family farewell.

It was not long before a new man surfaced in her mother's life, and Nancy and her brother learned that Roderick C. Richards would become their new father. The lanky, dark-haired Richards had the perfect pedigree, having graduated from Cornell University Medical College in New York City, spent two years in pediatrics at Lenox Hill Hospital in New York—first as an intern and then as an assistant resident—and then returned to exclusive Westchester County to start a practice of his own.

His aristocratic looks, bushy eyebrows, and long, slender nose, coupled with the fact that he was a successful doctor with a burgeoning practice, made him a desirable catch to the young women in Susan's social circle. The son of Mr. and Mrs. Carroll P. Richards of Withington Road in the Westchester town of Scarsdale, Roderick had moved back to his hometown after completing his medical school education, frequently treating the sons and daughters of his high school chums.

His decision to return to Westchester County, settling in one of the wealthiest communities in the nation, was to have a major impact on his adopted daughter's life. While its reputation was that of an exclusive, even snobbish, enclave of bluebloods and upper-crust WASPs, the tone of this upscale community was actually set in the seventeenth century.

According to local historians, Scarsdale was founded by

Caleb Heathcote, a sixth son born in 1666 to the family of Mayor Heathcote of Chesterfield in the Hundred of Scarsdale, Derbyshire, England. He was engaged to marry at the age of twenty-six, but his intended wife had turned her affections to one of Caleb's older brothers. Disappointed, he set sail for New York. A tradesman, he became one of the most successful men of the colony and began to buy up land in Westchester. By 1701, Heathcote established a royal manor, on land purchased with permission from William III, King of England, Scotland, France and Ireland, that he named Scarsdale for his ancestral home.

In the late nineteenth century, bankers and industrialists discovered the town. Scarsdale became the site of sprawling country homes and large estates of brick and stone, mansions complete with carriage houses and stables for the owners' prized Thoroughbreds. But over time, wealthy city dwellers, looking for serenity and a safe place to raise their families, discovered the countrified community, with its winding roads and eighteenth century homes. Soon, sparkling white houses with manicured shrubs and tended gardens dotted the landscape. Sycamores, elms, and maples lined the narrow, winding streets, a village dotted with country clubs and equestrian centers. Stately stone walls reminiscent of the English countryside encircled the larger properties along two-lane Mamaroneck Road. Scarsdale had more residents in the upper income brackets than most other comparable communities in the country, making it the most desirable—and most expensive—suburb in New York State.

Nancy's new father had spent his childhood not far from the exclusive golf clubs that served the area's wealthy patrons. In the 1950s, when Nancy and her family relocated to Dr. Richards' hometown, it had a population of just over thirteen thousand. Families with young children were drawn to the area for its fine public schools and close proximity to Manhattan.

Despite the idyllic setting of Nancy's childhood, the split between her mother and biological father caused a wound that would not heal. She never lost the hope of seeing her birth father again. But over time, she grew to fancy the kind, soft-spoken man whom she now called "Dad." A quiet, serious man who liked to be around kids, Dr. Richards immediately moved to adopt his fiancée's children and make them his own.

And while her relationship with Roderick Richards grew stronger with time, it was no secret that Nancy did not get on particularly well with her mother. She would later recount to friends Susan Richards' mood swings, and how she grew up feeling anxious in their wake.

For Nancy and her brother, change was everywhere. Susan chose to be married in an Episcopal Church because, as a divorcée, getting married in the Catholic Church was out of the question. Subsequently, the family moved to a new house, a sprawling Tudor on a private, residential street at 5 Brookline Drive. The enormous, three-storied white home with the dark wood trim was one of forty houses in an elite housing development called Sherbrooke Park. The quiet collection of intertwining streets with names such as Pinecrest and Locust was just off the main road, and not far from the commercial district where Dr. Richards' office was located. The house spanned an entire corner of Brookline Drive, and was bedecked with flourishing dogwood trees, rhododendron plants, and neatly pruned azalea bushes. From the tall French windows that faced the front of the house, the children could see the impressive Georgian stone estate and the outsized white-shingled residence of their neighbors across the street. A screened-in porch in the rear of the house, decoratively hung with flowering plants, afforded the family views of the woodsy area and stream outside their door. Inside, her mother's impressive personal library filled a large bookcase.

While it was no secret in the neighborhood that Dr. Richards had adopted Nancy and her younger brother, the circumstances that led to the adoption were shrouded in mystery—at least to the public. When Nancy's mother first began dating the pediatrician, it was big news on Garth Road, the busy commercial street in downtown Scarsdale where the doctor practiced. After taking their children to see the doctor at Eton Hall, the apartment building where Dr. Richards had his office, young mothers customarily pushed their baby strollers along the busy street and gossiped about the events and lives of those living in the small, exclusive neighborhood. One of their favorite topics was the new woman in Dr. Richards' life. Word was circulating that the eligible bachelor had taken up with the mother of two young children, and before long, news that he had asked her to be his wife was spreading like wildfire.

Neighbors of the new family believed that Nancy's biological father had passed away, clearing the way for Dr. Richards to assume parental responsibility when he married the "widowed" Susan Rehm. It was a story that Nancy repeated during the course of her life—even as an adult.

Nancy quickly grew to love her new father. To her, he was kind and gentle-hearted, and like her maternal grandparents, he only wanted the best for her. And besides, he was the only father that Nancy had ever really known. Dr. Richards was equally fond of his new daughter. He took a genuine interest in her pursuits, and delighted her with his repeated praise of her skill as a ballerina. She liked that he applauded her impromptu backyard performances and that he teasingly referred to her as the girl with "special dancing feet." But in spite of her close relationship with Dr. Richards, Nancy continued to wonder about her biological father. She would later tell friends that her adoptive father had been a stabilizing force in her life. She added that he was often compliant when it came to her mother, allowing Susan Richards to rule the roost, and rarely challenging her on issues both large and small.

In the years before her death, she tried to reestablish a relationship with her birth father. She confided to friends that on several occasions she had telephoned him, but had been hurt by his blasé attitude toward her. She was also disturbed by the sound of ice tinkling in a glass during their conversations, leading her to suspect that he may have had a drinking problem.

Nevertheless, she told one confidante that she remained angry with her mother for insisting that her father relinquish custody of her and her brother, and furious that her father had actually agreed to it. She interpreted his decision to comply with Susan Rehm's request as an outright rejection of her and John, and spent much of her life trying to make sense of it. But she never succeeded and remained both angry and sad about the circumstances of her early life until the day she died.

To Nancy, her father had, plainly and simply, abandoned his children, and she and her brother were the victims of his decision. Only after Nancy's death, more than four decades later, would her mother acknowledge her own culpability in making a decision that was so harmful to her children. Mrs. Richards eventually confessed to Nancy's friends that her first husband was not a monster. His only *real* crime, she revealed, was that he had not been a good match for her. But there was more. Mrs. Richards would later confide that her decision to end her marriage to Nancy's birth father had more to do with his inability to commit to her and their children. She spoke of sleepless nights sitting at home tending to Nancy and John Jr. while the children's father was out on the town, sometimes not returning to their residence until the following morning.

Whispers of her husband's all-night outings began to circulate among members of her elite crowd, and after careful consideration, Mrs. Richards decided it best to rid herself of her husband and go it alone. It was a painful choice and one that she knew would most definitely impact her two young children. But she also knew that she could not live her life this way, and needed to maintain her self-respect.

At the time, she honestly believed that removing her husband from her life and the lives of her children was the right thing to do. It was what young women of society did in those days. For many women in her clique, it was unheard of to keep the lines of communication open between an ex-husband and his children. In hindsight, Nancy's mother remorsefully regretted her decision.

When Nancy was nine years old, she learned that she was going to be a big sister for a second time. Her new brother, Roderick Clark Richards, Jr., the only son born to Susan and Roderick Richards, joined the family in 1961. Nancy's mother was in her mid-thirties when her youngest son was born, and Roderick was several years older.

Fair-haired and round of face, the adorable baby did not resemble either Nancy or her brother John, both of whom had angular features and thick, inky black hair. For Nancy, her thick tresses became a source of great anxiety as she struggled to fit in with and be accepted by the other children in her elementary and later, her junior high school classes. With pin-straight hair all the rage, she was often frustrated and self-conscious of her wild mane of curls. The young girl hated how she looked, and wanted to do anything she could to straighten her tresses. Even more frustrating were the short bobs that she was forced to wear, deemed necessary by her mother to keep her unwieldy locks looking manicured and neat.

The following year, Nancy began the sixth grade at Scarsdale Junior High School. The large tan-brick schoolhouse on busy Mamaroneck Road was set back from the street, and its floor-to-ceiling windows, decorated with drawings and cut-outs made by the students, looked out onto a field of rolling green grass.

Several afternoons a week, Nancy attended ballet lessons at a local dance studio and for a while, she dreamed of becoming a ballerina. She spent hours choreographing her own dance routines, and liked to perform them to imaginary audiences in her basement and in the family's grassy backyard. Other days, she headed straight for home where she and her brother took turns walking the family dog. Neighbors on the block were taken aback by the strange, high-pitched whooping sound that Nancy and other members of her family made when they wanted to call the family's big German Shepherd back into the house.

Yet while Nancy and her family lived a life that was typical of the 1950s, their neighbors sensed that beneath the façade of tranquility, there were problems in the Richards' household. While Dr. Richards maintained a successful pediatric practice, was a regular at the country club, and was an accepted member of the highest social circles, people buzzed about how peculiar he was. To many, he seemed disconnected, and unusually "laid back," and his unflappable demeanor seemed odd to those who imagined that a doctor had the weight of the world—or at least the weighty problems of his patients—on his mind.

Nancy's mother, meanwhile, was viewed as cold, distant and overly proper, even by Scarsdale standards. Her remoteness was keenly felt by Nancy, who later confided to friends that she never quite knew how her mother really felt about her. While she recalled spending countless hours on her mother's lap, listening as storybook after storybook was read to her, her mother's aloofness left her questioning how deeply she loved her. Nancy did not understand her mother's lack of emotion and spontaneity, and as children tend to do, she interpreted these deficiencies as something that was lacking in her.

An active member of the Junior League, she participated in countless fundraisers and other charitable events considered worthy by her upper crust crowd. She was known for her social etiquette and tasteful dress, which she carried over to her daughter, who she dressed in pricey, well-tailored clothes. But young Nancy was forever frustrated by the lack of color in her wardrobe, and resented that all of her outfits were either navy, gray or black. If the choice had been up to her, she would have preferred bolder, more fashionable ensembles, and she secretly dreamed of the day her mother would buy her a cherry red overcoat.

Family friends believe that Nancy's brothers also found it a challenge to relate to their mother. Both boys were viewed as loners, and her older brother John had earned a social reputation as being an undesirable playmate for other children in the community.

The peculiarities of the family, as well as a need to escape the unbearable pain of having lost a parent, may have accounted for Nancy's self-professed tendency to daydream for hours on end. As an adult, she would speak of childhood years spent fantasizing all sorts of imaginary scenarios and spinning endless tales of romance and love. In her stories, the hero did not walk away from his beloved, like her own father had done. Instead, he remained true to a fault, launching a fight so fierce to protect his loved one that nothing less than triumph was even considered.

Eventually, her overactive imagination would lead her to a successful career as an author of historical romances. Her first writings would be as editor of *The Cauldron*, the literary magazine of the prominent East Coast boarding school she would attend in pastoral New England. At fourteen, Nancy learned she was to spend the next four years at the Kent School in northwestern Connecticut. Her paternal grandfather, John Rehm, was to foot the bill for her boarding school tuition, schoolbooks, and any other expenses his darling Nancy incurred.

Founded just after the turn of the century, the distinguished educational institution was rooted in Episcopal history. Its founding father, Frederick H. Sil, was an Episcopal minister ordained by the Order of the Holy Cross. His mission as headmaster of what was then an all-boys' institution was to teach simplicity of life, directness of purpose, and self-reliance. Enrollment was limited to students with exemplary academic qualifications as well as a track record as good citizens.

Father Sil was a true anglophile—so much so that his decision to build the Kent School in the valley town of Kent, Connecticut, was based in large part on its striking resemblance to his beloved England. While searching for a site, Father Sil had been wandering the northwest section of Connecticut when he happened upon the tiny summer resort town. A two-hour train ride from New York's Grand Central Terminal, it had become popular with well-heeled city dwellers anxious to escape the metropolis' sultry summer temperatures. But the off-season conditions were what really captured Father Sil's attention. The mist rolling off of craggy Mt. Algo conjured images of Great Britain. An even bigger selling point was that the town was situated on the banks of the Housatonic River, which would be a prime site for a crew team to train and compete.

Some believe that the school's Anglo-influence may have played a role in Nancy's later interest in the writing of Regency romance novels. For instance, components of Father Sil's own family crest were incorporated into the school's insignia, and a crew team was immediately assembled and, to this day, continues to be the Kent School's leading athletic activity. As headmaster of the Kent School, Father Sil retained much of the British culture, choosing to set aside the American class system in favor of the British "forms." At Kent, students attending the ninth grade are referred to as "sixth classmen," and so on. Boys were required to attend classes in a coat and tie, and when women came on the scene in 1959, the dress code consisted of school uniforms.

Just off Macedonia Road, a dignified Civil War monument, reminiscent of the statues dotting English villages, sits in the center of town and the one-hundred-acre boys' campus, with its Georgian-style buildings, lies directly in the path of the Appalachian Trail.

When Nancy's parents enrolled their daughter at Kent School, it had a reputation as a leading liberal arts institution, and registering there was said to help motivated students gain acceptance to Ivy League colleges and universities. It was ranked just below top-notch institutions such as Andover and Exeter. The curriculum was a general high school program of arts, sciences, and mathematics, but there was also another, more important element. Students were taught to be socially conscious through participation in a variety of volunteer and charitable activities.

The grounds of the Kent School for Girls, known simply as G-S, was abloom with a carpet of red and purple wildflowers when Nancy arrived for her first semester in the fall of 1965. And while she felt some sense of relief to be getting away from her mother's moodiness, she was soon confronted by the realities of boarding school life. The decades-old institution wasn't always easy for the teenager who later expressed feeling that she had been "dispatched" from the family upon her enrollment at the campus. Living away from home in a stark dormitory, and sharing a room with several other girls, was sometimes difficult, and eating meal after meal in a windowless, rectangular dining hall that could be drafty and dark in the dead of winter was also a trial.

It was no secret that dining cafeteria-style at lengthy wooden tables, under a life-size oil painting of Father Sil, was hardly a substitute for the intimacy of family meals around the kitchen table. It wasn't that the dining room was unpleasant. On the contrary, its lofty ceilings, expansive stone fireplace, and the dark wood walls, hung with colorful pennants representing various club teams, captured an atmosphere of Old World England. But in the cold, snowy months of December and January, the sun would go down behind the snow-capped Mt. Algo as early as four-thirty in the afternoon, casting eerie shadows on the campus from the barren tree limbs and heavily mullioned architecture. The early sunset would cause the air temperature to suddenly plummet, and the atmosphere in the valley could be both dismal and damp.

Even more trying were the ten-minute bus rides from the Girls' School down the steep hill to the main campus each morning. Since the classrooms were located at the boys' campus on Macedonia Road, Nancy and the other girls had no choice but to travel the narrow, dizzying Skiff Mountain Road, with dramatic drops on both sides. On icy days, the journey could be most treacherous, with students closing their eyes and clutching the seat in front of them.

In keeping with Father Sil's vision of developing self-sufficiency, Nancy and her classmates were expected to perform various chores around the campus, such as clearing the dinner plates and cleaning the grounds. Students were also obligated to attend services at St. Joseph's Chapel six days a week, and twice on Sundays. The impressive stone church was modeled in the British tradition and topped by an authentic bell tower. Instruction on how to use the tower was also part of the curriculum and a requirement of all students at the school.

Weekends were primarily for studying, but there was also time set aside for socializing. Dances with the prestigious neighboring schools of Trinity Pawling, Canterbury, Westminster, and Symsbury were held on Friday and Saturday evenings, and second-run movies were shown at the campus theater. Nancy and her friends particularly enjoyed the jaunts into Manhattan where students were treated to a day at the Metropolitan Museum of Art or other cultural institutions. On holidays, Nancy headed home for Scarsdale.

While some might have chafed under the regimentation, Nancy enjoyed her time at the Kent School. She found the orderliness comforting, especially after the emotional chaos she had experienced at home. She thrived amidst her newfound independence and made a lot of friends.

Nancy's penchant for writing also blossomed during her years at Kent. She was senior editor of the *Kent News*, which was published every six weeks, and editor of *The Cauldron*, the school's literary magazine. Her love of words extended into dramatics, a passion she contemplated pursuing professionally. She learned later in life that other Kent School graduates had followed this path, including Ted Danson, star of the television sitcom *Cheers*, who graduated the year before she arrived.

Acting was a talent that came naturally to Nancy, and she liked to showcase her abilities in the company of friends. Without prompting, she would teasingly assume other voices, or break into theatrical performances to dramatize a point she was trying to make. Her giddy role-playing kept her friends in stitches, and in later years, helped her to interject a little fun when life became too serious to bear. Her style of dress was equally theatrical. While the other girls shed their plaid uniforms on weekends to don sweater sets, turtlenecks, and slacks, Nancy preferred a more "Jacqueline Kennedy" look, which included large-framed sunglasses and a colorful scarf to encircle her neck.

As a member of the Thespian Society, she befriended Richard "Treat" Williams. The talented actor burst on the film scene playing the role of a New York police detective turned justice department informant in the 1981 film *Prince of the City*. He also played Stanley Kowalski in a made-for-television version of *A Streetcar Named Desire* in 1984.

Raised in nearby Rowayton, Connecticut, "Treat" was a member of Nancy's graduating class. During her last year at Kent, he had a very small role in the school's production of *The American Dream*, in which she played the part of Mommie. The same year, she also landed the starring role as Antigone in Sophocles' Greek tragedy of the same name. Her performance was the grand finale of four years spent at the exclusive boarding school, and she received a standing ovation from her high school peers.

Her summers were spent touring the world with her wealthy maternal grandparents, who included such cosmopolitan cities as Paris, London, and Rome on the whirlwind itinerary. Her trips were fully funded by Grandma and Grandpa Rehm, who wanted only the best for their darling Nancy. From the moment her grandfather laid eyes on her, his affection for her never waned. The two enjoyed countless hours together, talking and joking about every subject imaginable.

The wealthy businessman spared no expense when it came to his granddaughter, and his generosity included an all-out extravaganza for her sixteenth birthday. The Holly Ball, also known as "the biggest social event of the season," was the elegant debutante party held each summer at the ritzy Scarsdale Golf Club in nearby Hartsdale. For sixteen-year-old Nancy, a celebration on the same scale marked her debut into society, and she counted it among the highlights of her young and privileged life. Her coming out was topped off by a whirlwind trip around the world with her grandparents, who over the years had taken Nancy to the far corners of the earth in first-class style.

But upon her return, Nancy was forced to confront the difficulties her family continued to grapple with, even in her absence. And while boarding school afforded Nancy the opportunity to escape from the emotional turmoil, her younger brother John was not as lucky. Unlike his sister, John had never really adjusted to the changes that had taken place early in his life.

His difficulties continued throughout his teens. His troublesome behavior landed him at a special school—in spite of the fact that his father, Dr. Richards, had signed on as the doctor for the Scarsdale school system in 1969 when John turned fifteen.

Of the three, Roderick fared the best, perhaps because he had never experienced the wrenching separation his half-brother and half-sister had when they were children.

Nancy's youngest brother—who was known to his friends as "Rod" "Rodder" and "Dor"—was a loner, which was perhaps his own way of coping with the instability at home. Classmates described Roderick Jr. as very much his own person, someone who never cared much about being part of a group. One of the tallest members of the Scarsdale Boys' Cross-Country team, the gangly teen with the wide smile and thin mustache looked very much like his father. He wore his shoulder-length, light-brown hair brushed to one side, and his quiet, serious demeanor was often mistaken for snobbery. Unlike Nancy, he weathered the emotional ups and downs at home with a fair degree of equanimity, and graduated from Scarsdale High School exactly ten years after she completed her education at the exclusive boarding school in northwest Connecticut.

Nancy had proudly walked the lawn of the Kent School for the last time in June of 1969, her dark eyes hidden behind large-framed sunglasses, her thick locks of chocolate-brown hair tucked neatly behind her ears. Amidst the lilac and cherry trees that were in full bloom, she received her high school diploma on Prize Day, the name given to the school's commencement exercises and the awards ceremony that followed.

Her next stop would be Washington, DC and the gated campus of exclusive Mt. Vernon College. It was a move that would bring her professional success. It would also bring Jeremy Akers into her life.

CHAPTER EIGHT

THE STIFLING, MUGGY DAYS OF SUMMER IN THE DISTRICT of Columbia were giving way to September's more temperate climate when Nancy arrived in the Capital City for her first day of classes at Mt. Vernon College. The private women's school she had chosen to attend had a reputation as a "debutante" college, and was popular with the daughters of well-heeled families, and of Washington's ambassadors and diplomats.

After four isolated winters spent at the remote New England boarding school, Nancy enjoyed the hustle-bustle of big city living and the intimate atmosphere of the small, well-secured campus. She and her fellow classmates felt secure behind its scrolling wire gates, and protected by the twenty-four-hour manned security booth located at the school's front entrance. It was here that she befriended the woman who would remain one of her closest friends. From the moment that Nancy met Alison Van Meter, the two became instant friends. Their bond remained strong even after Nancy transferred to another college, with Alison serving as Nancy's maid of honor at her runaway wedding to the man who would ultimately take her life.

Mt. Vernon College was situated in the heart of downtown DC, steps from young and trendy Georgetown, and gorgeous cherry and maple trees surrounded its Federal-style brick buildings. Nancy was attending college at a volatile time in our nation's history. The Vietnam War was

escalating overseas and she watched protesters descending
on the White House almost daily. The boys in her own
social circle were choosing to stay clear of the Vietnam
conflict, opting instead to study at Ivy League undergrad-
uate and graduate schools.

Nancy continued to excel in the areas of history and
English during her two years at the small liberal arts college, and living in the nation's capital also provided her
with an insider's view of the political arena. It was nearly
impossible for anybody living in the District to avoid getting pulled in to the daily controversies that raged over the
war. Nancy was among them, and her escalating interest in
world affairs ultimately led her to change her major from
English to international studies.

In many ways, it seemed that she was like a chameleon,
able to adapt and change effortlessly to any situation. She
had already adjusted to life with a new father and to the
demands of a rigorous private school. In the years to come,
she would exhibit an unerring ability to transform herself
to fill a number of roles.

On weekends, she and her classmates took advantage of
the city's cosmopolitan social scene, attending dances and
parties teeming with young college men enrolled at George
Washington and Georgetown universities, both of which
were considered "dating schools" by the women of Mt.
Vernon College.

Sunday mornings were often spent at Clyde's of Georgetown, the popular hangout where students congregated to
sip Bloody Marys and gobble down Eggs Benedict.

Nancy's roommate was employed as a hostess at the M
Street eatery and was assigned to work the busy Sunday
morning shift. It was a perfect reason for Nancy to join her
there to grab a quick bite and partake in the festivities before returning to the dorm for an afternoon of study. It was

there at Clyde's that she was introduced to Bill Ranger, a Georgetown University student and part-time waiter at the eatery whom she would later meet as one of her future husband's closest friends.

In the fall of 1971, Nancy transferred to Sweet Briar College, the top-notch women's liberal arts school in the rolling green hills of Sweet Briar, Virginia. The expansive campus covered 3,300 acres of Virginia's Wine Country, and was set at the foothills of the breathtaking Blue Ridge Mountains, about twelve miles north of Lynchburg, one hour south of Charlottesville, and 150 miles southwest of Washington, DC.

Like Mt. Vernon College, Nancy was aware that Sweet Briar College was considered a debutante way station, and was attended by wealthy "society" girls, many of whom went on to gain financial wherewithal by marrying prominent politicians and businessmen. In a school with only six hundred students, and fewer than twelve pupils to a class, individual attention abounded at the tiny institution that had a reputation as one of the finest four-year colleges in the nation. The intimate classroom settings promoted greater interaction among the students and their professors, and afforded Sweet Briar enrollees with a level of education unrivaled by private colleges in its class.

In addition to its academics, students on the beautiful campus enjoyed excellent accommodations with all of the amenities of a first-class hotel and a panoramic view of the Virginia countryside. There were two lakes for fishing and swimming, trails and nature sanctuaries for hiking, walking, and jogging, two athletic fields, fourteen tennis courts, and an Olympic-sized pool. Sweet Briar women also had access to the famed Harriet Howell Rogers Riding Center, an equestrian facility renowned as the best-designed college facility in the country.

Nancy and her classmates particularly enjoyed walking the campus' national historic district, which is comprised of sixteen of the school's original structures, red-brick buildings designed with A-shaped slate roofs and spectacular views of the Blue Ridge mountains. Among the structures was the gracious Sweet Briar House, the original mansion of the college's founder. For Nancy, attending classes in the historic buildings—designed in part by Thomas Jefferson, whose Monticello was located not far from the campus—was preferable to the more contemporary buildings that had been added on over the years.

The chronic daydreamer—who, as a child, fantasized about a career as a ballet dancer, and as a teen was determined to become an actress—declared a major in government studies, one of two academic programs for which the school was well-known. Her choice of study was a far cry from the creative pursuits in which she had participated over the past twenty years, and would take her in a direction that she had never intended for herself.

On May 20, 1973, Nancy graduated with a Bachelor of Arts in government, and, at twenty-two, returned to Washington, DC to pursue a career in her field of expertise. Her jobs were varied and prestigious. They ranged from speechwriter for Sam Ervin, senator from North Carolina, to researcher for the Senate Foreign Relations Committee on the Salt II Treaties that were never ratified. In addition, she worked for the Democratic National Committee.

She had been employed on "the Hill" for nearly three years when she was introduced to the person who would soon become her husband. Jeremy Ray Akers was like no other man she had ever dated. The well-built Southerner with the throaty voice and thick drawl had a feral manner that set him apart from the polished boarding school boys of her past. Nancy found the disposition of the hard little man with the strawberry-blonde hair and solid gold eye-tooth a welcome change from the staid and conservative style of her former boyfriends. He was not only charming—he was fun.

It excited her that Jeremy had served his country in the United States Marine Corps, and that he was decorated for his heroic acts during the Vietnam War. She had never dated a man who counted alligator hunting among his favorite pastimes, and she was enamored not only with his physical strength, but also with his excessively polite manner and dapper, Southern style. She liked that he took time to help the elderly and went out of his way to lend a hand to single women and young mothers in need. And that he was so incredibly loyal to his country, and to his family, all of which made her proud to be by his side.

To Nancy, Jeremy was the most exciting person she had ever encountered, and from their very first date she was determined to make him hers. She was aware that his upbringing greatly differed from her own, but that was part of what made him so appealing. She was struck by his discipline and self-control, which was reflected even in the way he dressed. Before leaving the house, he spent an inordinate amount of time in front of a full-length mirror, tying and retying his tie and scrutinizing his pants for creases and wrinkles. His closet was meticulously ordered, with like items neatly hung side by side. He adored ties, and had a tremendous collection that he agonized over before making a decision.

But there was something wild and untamed about Jeremy Akers, and for Nancy the combination of his qualities was irresistible. She was convinced that as staff counsel to the House Select Committee on Assassinations, the poised, intelligent attorney was on the fast track to success. And while her parents did not approve of her new boyfriend,

her friends could not help but notice how she lit up whenever he was around.

To casual acquaintances, Jeremy carried himself as
though he was a member of the Southern aristocracy. His
courtly manner and controlled steadiness gave him an air
of class and sophistication. But those who knew him better
sensed that inwardly, he was self-conscious and uncomfortable about his humble beginnings and longed for something more. In the rough-and-tumble world of Washington
politics, having the right woman on his arm was important
to Jeremy, and he gravitated toward women like Nancy
who commanded respect.

Yet, while Jeremy found the shapely, dark-haired
speechwriter attractive, he had no intention of giving up his
bachelorhood, and continued dating as many women as he
could fit into his schedule. He still could not believe that
he had attained this lifestyle, appointed to such an important
role, re-creating himself as a prominent DC lawyer who
was working on Capitol Hill, winning the respect of his
colleagues. Women considered him worldly and polished,
and he suddenly found himself in the position of having
his pick of Washington's most desirable dates. It was almost too much for a small-town boy to have ever imagined.

While his new love interest was telling her friends that
she would not date anyone but Jeremy, he was out on the
town with other women. He did little to hide his disinterest
in a more serious commitment, and he even let it be known
that he was dating around. Nevertheless, during the time he
did spend with Nancy, he was overbearing and controlling,
even advising her to quit her position with the Democratic
National Committee because he didn't like the Party's politics: Nancy, who would do anything to keep him interested, strove to please him. Although brilliant and
competent, Nancy seemed to lack the self-esteem necessary

to disagree with the man she considered her handsome hero. Eager to please, she eventually agreed to leave her post with the DNC to make the new object of her affections happy. But her devotion and compliance did little to bring Jeremy closer to making a commitment to her.

In fact, his desire to cool things down did not sit well with Nancy, who seemed almost addicted to his volatile disposition. She found herself attracted to the characteristics that made other women on the Hill shy away from Jeremy. To them, his sardonic humor and intense, dark personality translated into something dangerous. To Nancy, they were the qualities that magnetized her.

When she finally agreed to separate, Jeremy's friends couldn't understand why Nancy continued to take Jeremy back even though she knew that he had been unfaithful, or why she continued to look the other way when it was clear that he had taken up with yet another young lady. While most women would have taken his indiscretions to heart, Nancy remained strangely true to Jeremy, penning him love letters, and believing that ultimately he would see his way back to her. For a woman who had been abandoned in childhood by her father, perhaps she continued to set herself up for some kind of rejection or future abandonment.

"Opposites attract" might be the simple explanation for why Nancy found Jeremy so attractive. It is not uncommon for the athlete to be attracted to the couch potato or the intellectual to find comfort in the "street smarts" of a non-academic type. To a large degree, both Nancy and Jeremy were entranced with each other. Perhaps she found his kind of rigid discipline and focused, goal-setting style a complement to her own innate creativity and her tendency to dreaminess and fantasy. And maybe he found her free spirit and wild side a complement to his own uptightness.

Yet, when Jeremy announced that he was leaving town

for Colorado to join his former law school roommate, Ron Castille, at the ski camp he was running for military amputees, Nancy was heartbroken—another abandonment. She listened in disbelief as he told her that his departure would mark the end of their relationship. To her, the idea of losing Jeremy was completely unacceptable, and she resolved to win him back no matter what it was going to take.

Her determination—or desperation—prompted her to buy a plane ticket to the west, where she paid a surprise visit to the man she was desperately obsessed with. Her unannounced arrival stunned Jeremy, who was enjoying life as a ski bum in the opulent snow-capped playground of the rich and celebrated. While Nancy had literally chased after him countless times during their on-again, off-again relationship, this time her efforts yielded the results that she so urgently desired.

When Nancy announced that she was pregnant with the couple's first child, Jeremy quickly got down on bended knee and asked her to be his wife. Friends of the couple say that his proposal had less to do with the pregnancy and more to do with Jeremy's impulsive, sudden change of heart, perhaps influenced by his strong Christian values. Friends recall a conversation in which Nancy and Jeremy confided that their decision to marry was based on the belief that their union would ultimately be consummated in matrimony, and said that they agreed to keep their exact wedding date a secret in order to protect their first child from feeling awkward about their premarital relationship. In fact, it would not be until the day after Nancy's murder that their son, Finny, would learn through a newspaper article the true circumstances of his parents' nuptials.

Arrangements for a kind of "elopement"-style wedding were made quickly, with Nancy excitedly alerting only a handful of people, and asking Alison, her best girlfriend from her days at Mt. Vernon College, to be her maid of honor.

Jeremy, meanwhile, waited until the very last minute to invite a few close friends. In fact, he phoned one of his closet pals just a few hours before he was set to exchange his vows. Tom Turchan told one reporter that he was stunned when he answered the telephone to hear his long-time friend request that he, "Come to Christ Episcopal tonight at seven-thirty."

"I'm not coming until you tell me what is going on," Tom demanded.

"Turchan, I'm telling you to be there." Jeremy provided no other information.

It was only after a protracted conversation with a surreptitious Jeremy that Turchan heard his friend say, "I'm getting married."

Tom was astounded, and quickly hung up the phone to alert their friends in New York and Baltimore. When he got the other guys on the line, he could not believe that not a single one of them had received a call from Jeremy. It seemed that his friend had "forgotten" to tell anybody.

On August 11, 1977, Nancy slipped on the elegant wedding dress that she had borrowed from Alison. Her beautiful and generous friend had recently worn the stunning couture gown for her marriage to William Paley, Jr., grandson of media tycoon William S. Paley, the founder of the Columbia Broadcasting System (CBS).

Twenty-six years old, and four months pregnant, Nancy proudly clasped her bouquet, and effortlessly floated down the aisle of Georgetown's Christ Church. The magnificent Episcopal Church was located at 31st and O Street in the posh Northwest section of the city where, over the years, it had been the site of several prominent weddings.

Nancy smiled from behind her diaphanous white veil as she passed the small group of friends who lined the pews, and made her way to the altar, which was tastefully decorated with sprays of delicate flowers. As she strode down the aisle, her gaze was fixed on Jeremy, who waited stone-faced, his shoulders squared, his hands clasped tightly in front of him. His blank expression revealed nothing of what was going through his mind—or heart—as he watched his stunning bride approach, his eyes illuminated by the pair of tall, white candles that flickered in front of him at the altar. The resident minister performed the brief but moving ceremony, which ended in a passionate kiss and a round of applause from the couple's close friends.

Suddenly, Nancy had two secrets from her family: her marriage and her pregnancy. She had always lived up to her family's expectations, but now it was clear that she was embarking on a journey in which she would live two separate, even contradictory, lives.

For more than one month, she and Jeremy kept their nuptials concealed, until they matter-of-factly announced to their families that they had wed in an intimate church affair. Nancy's family received the news of their daughter's runaway marriage with regret. Her mother was less than pleased that the event had been shrouded in secrecy, and was having a difficult time believing that her daughter could really be in love with a man who fell so short of her own lofty expectations. Nine years her daughter's senior, Jeremy Ray Akers was not the kind of man Nancy's mother would have chosen for her. And she made it a point of letting him know it right from the start. One of the questions she asked him during their initial encounter was who his family was, a question that friends say made Jeremy feel self-conscious and unimportant. Susan Richards did not appreciate her son-in-law's abrasive manner, and found it more than disconcerting when he spoke to her with his face just inches away from her own. Something about her daughter's new husband raised concern in her, and she could not shake the vague and uneasy feeling that her daughter was somehow in danger. Nancy's brothers were equally turned off by their sister's choice. They found her new husband brash and opinionated, and over the years they became increasingly uncomfortable during visits to Nancy's home. They found Jeremy unpleasant and rude, and disliked that he went out of his way to make them feel unwelcome in their sister's house. Jeremy's relatives seemed to take the news in stride, and upon learning of the soon-to-be-born grandchild, embraced their son's pretty new bride with sincerity and delight.

Five months after they exchanged their nuptials on January 6, 1978, Nancy and Jeremy proudly welcomed their first son, Rehm Johnson Preston Akers. He was named for members of both Nancy's and Jeremy's families. His first name was for Nancy's maternal grandfather, John Rehm, and his second name was for a great-great uncle on Jeremy's side, Albert Sidney Johnston, who served as a general in the War Between the States. But, it was unrealistic to expect that people call the young boy by such a dignified, adult title, and he was instead nicknamed Finny, after his godfather's son.

Shortly after Finny celebrated his first birthday, Jeremy landed a very exciting job in Dade County, Florida. His impeccable and impressive credentials earned him a spot in the office of the state attorney. His position as Assistant State Attorney under Janet Reno promised an exciting career investigating, evaluating, preparing, and trying criminal cases. During Jeremy's four years with the office, he was assigned to the Economic Fraud Division, where he specialized in white-collar crime, political corruption, and food stamp and Medicare fraud. He also supervised and directed criminal investigative teams that consisted of law enforcement officers from the local police departments, state agencies, and the state attorney's office.

The family moved to a small Mediterranean-style house on a lovely residential street near the bay. The home, which was surrounded by palm trees and flowering bougainvillea, was located in chic Coconut Grove, a trendy hotspot on Florida's east coast. Just south of downtown Miami, the rambling tourist town was lined with expensive shops and stylish restaurants. The beautiful, upscale community was an ideal spot for Nancy to enjoy the outdoors. And the quiet, suburban streets provided a perfect setting for her to stroll with the baby carriage. Nancy later recalled this as one of the most idyllic times of her life, living in a beautiful house with a tile floor, lush vegetation, and great weather, surrounded by what seemed to be the perfect family.

Since she was not working, her time as a new mother gave her an opportunity to rediscover her love of painting and sketching. Finny benefited from his mother's creative flair, and enjoyed imaginative arts-and-crafts projects she designed for him and the afternoon outings to parks and museums they took. An avid reader, Nancy regaled her young son with storybook adventures. As a youngster, she put him to bed each night to the whimsical children's story, *Goodnight Moon* by Margaret Wise Brown. The fantastical tale of the little white rabbit preparing for bedtime was her baby boy's favorite, although he also became attached to a number of the books in his library of fairy tales and adventures during the course of his childhood.

On weekends, Nancy and Jeremy packed a bag and took their young son on hikes through the park, stopping by the playground to watch, whoop, and holler as he zoomed down the slide or played on the jungle gym. Nancy shared her husband's love of the outdoors, and the couple took Finny on countless adventures, including a magical journey through the Everglades. Nancy even indulged her husband's love of exotic animals, embracing the pair of parrots and the gigantic macaw that he brought home for his son. Over time, the family's collection of pets grew to a menagerie of dogs, cats, fish, mice, birds, and even a few snakes that Jeremy had found on his long hikes. And while she would have preferred to be the owner of a single cat or dog, Nancy held her tongue and simply smiled at each new pet her husband added to the constantly growing collection.

Being the first and only grandchild in his mother's family, and the first baby born to Gladys and William Akers' eldest son, Finny was in great demand. Every summer, Nancy and Jeremy arranged for their little boy to visit with his grandparents in Sheffield. It was a journey that the youngster looked forward to for much of the year. The slender, dark-haired toddler with the mop of corkscrew curls adored his father's parents, and counted his trips to their quaint, rural Southern town among the highlights of his young life.

The fact that Grandpa Bill was retired from his job with the railroad meant that he was home and free to dote on his darling grandson twenty-four hours a day. Finny also spent time with a host of relatives from his dad's side, and learned all about the family members for whom he was named. And for one week, Nancy and Jeremy joined their son in Alabama at a vacation house on the lake that the elder Akerses rented in nearby Muscle Shoals.

Being away for most of the summer meant that Finny was unable to see his grandparents and his great grandparents on his mother's side. Desperate to spend time with their precious Finny, Roderick and Susan Richards made frequent trips to visit with the family during the winter months. It became customary for them to fly down to their daughter's home to celebrate Thanksgiving with their grandson, and then to host the family at their stately mansion in Scarsdale for extended Christmas holidays at which Nancy's beloved grandfather, John Rehm, got the opportunity to dote on his great grandson.

While Nancy adored Jeremy's family, and looked forward to her visits to Alabama, her husband did not feel as loving toward her family. She was aware that he was uncomfortable in their presence, and he showed little enthusiasm when she announced that they were coming to stay. She knew that he found it difficult to control his tongue around her mother, and tried her best to keep Susan Richards at bay.

The Akers family was in sunny Florida only a short time when Jeremy stumbled upon his old law school pal, Don Boswell. The young attorney was aware that his friend had moved to Florida after graduating from the University of Virginia, but he never dreamed of running into him in the lobby of the Miami courthouse.

Don was equally shocked when he heard the deep, baritone voice of his former law school roommate clear across the corridor. But what really caught Don's attention was his pal's outrageous getup. In spite of his conservative views, Jeremy had never been one to follow trends, and on this day, his fashion statement reinforced that notion.

Anxiously, Don shouted Jeremy's name across the sunny passageway, and then watched as the slender, blond-haired man in the canary-yellow pants and red suspenders turned to see who was calling him. When he recognized his friend's familiar grin, he excitedly ran over to shake his buddy's hand. It had been nearly five years since they last spoke. Don and Jeremy had lost touch soon after Jeremy left Charlottesville for California. Since neither man was adept at writing or sending holiday cards, reuniting in the busy downtown courthouse was a welcome surprise.

Delighted at the good fortune of coming upon Don after all the preceding years, Jeremy insisted that their fateful meeting be toasted with a celebratory drink. Happily, Don agreed, and the two headed off to a local tavern to down a few beers and catch up on old times. News that his pal had gotten married and had a son came as a shock to Don, since he never considered Jeremy the marrying kind.

When Jeremy proposed that they stop by his house so that he could introduce Don to his new wife and young son, he willingly obliged. He was curious to meet the woman who had agreed to marry his nutty friend, and was surprised by the intelligent, free-spirited person he encountered when he arrived at the spacious house near the bay. Not only was Nancy attractive and smart, but Don also found his friend's wife funny, artistic, and incredibly kind. She was well-read and could talk for hours about everything from the classics to free verse. She was also, Don noted, artistic, with real talent in painting and drawing. Pleased by his interest, Nancy proudly exhibited some of her recent works for Don.

Over the next several years, Don and Nancy grew to be friends. A consummate bachelor, Jeremy's old pal liked to stop over for dinner every few months, and enjoyed taking Nancy and young Finny out for cruises on his sailboat. But Don stopped short of making his dinner visits routine. After all, he was single, and did not want to impose himself on Jeremy and his family.

During one conversation that he had with Nancy, Don was surprised to learn that she had been the one to pursue his old law school pal. He was even more taken aback when she spoke about Jeremy as though he fit some romantic profile she had conjured up in her head. Don had never viewed his friend as the romantic type, and he certainly never expected Jeremy to turn up with a wife and a child.

After five years with the office of the state attorney, Jeremy was offered the opportunity of a lifetime, and he excitedly raced home to tell Nancy that he had been asked to come on board as a trial lawyer for the United States Department of Justice in the nation's capital.

It was a dream come true—not only for Jeremy, who was about to begin the kind of job he had always aspired to, but also for Nancy. She relished the idea of returning to the city where she not only had spent glorious days as a student, but had also launched her own career as a political speechwriter. Neither Nancy nor Jeremy had any inkling that their move to Washington, DC would set them on a path that would ultimately prove deadly.

CHAPTER NINE

AT FORTY-ONE YEARS OLD, JEREMY HAD REACHED THE pinnacle of his legal career. As a trial attorney for the United States Department of Justice, he was assigned to the Environmental Enforcement Section of the department's environment and natural resources division. It was an area that he found most rewarding and was exhilarated at the prospect of working on assignments that could potentially make a significant impact on the environment.

Among his duties, he was responsible for the investigation, evaluation, preparation, negotiation, and trial of cases arising under federal environmental statutes. During his five years with the Department, he worked on the Comprehensive Environmental Response, Compensation and Liability Act ("CERCLA" or "Superfund"), the Resource Conservation and Recovery Act, the Toxic Substances Control Act, the Federal Water Pollution Control Act, the Clean Air Act, and the Federal Insecticide Fungicide, and Rodenticide Act.

At first, the couple rented a lovely Tudor-style townhouse in Foxhall Village on 44th Street, barely a mile from Georgetown in the trendy northwest section of the city. The brown and cream-colored semi-detached residence was part of an upscale housing complex and was inhabited by a number of young, upwardly mobile families.

Neighbors on the lovely tree-lined street remember Nancy had a kind of movie-star quality. Shapely and attractive, her presence was imposing. She was larger than life with her thick, dark hair pulled tightly in a bun, and the oversized sunglasses she wore even when it was raining gave her an air of glamour. Her outfits were always colorful and modern, and she accented them with whimsical scarves slung loosely around her throat. Her style was that of a modified hippie, with billowy, multi-hued ensembles and fashionable, chunky-heeled shoes.

Physical appearance was important to Nancy. While she gave the impression of being very much a bohemian-style woman, she made sure never to miss her monthly facial appointment at Elizabeth Arden, or her weekly manicures and pedicures at the local salon. Her clothing, for the most part, bore the fancy Laura Ashley label, and she made it clear that she would rather own one dress with her favorite designer's name than ten items that were "off the rack."

Residents of the block found Nancy's husband equally charismatic. Handsome and athletic, the short, well-toned man was often seen taking Finny to the nearby park on Q Street, where the father and son would practice baseball, toss a Frisbee or fly a kite. Once there, Jeremy seemed unable to resist joining the local boys in a game of hoops. Securing his young son on a park bench, he always pulled off his T-shirt to reveal a chest of muscles that impressed even the youngsters on the court. He seemed to like to run around shirtless while playing ball with whoever was in the park. One of the boys, eleven-year-old Avery Drake, passed the Akers place twice a day on his way to and from school. He immediately recognized the man with the bulging biceps and pumped-up physique as the same person he always saw doing yard work or tinkering with his car.

Now that Nancy was back in the District of Columbia, and her son was of school age, she realized that she would have to return to the workforce. It was clear to her that her husband's government salary would not go far in the Capital City, where rents were high and everyday life was expensive. And Nancy was determined to send Finny to private school, and had been informed by Jeremy that she would be responsible for footing the steep tuition bill. Her husband believed in public education, and made it clear to Nancy that if she wanted five-year-old Finny to go to private school, she would have to pay for it herself. For Nancy, the idea of enrolling her son in the District's public school system was not an option. Education was her highest priority and she was well aware that the public schools were less than the ideal environment for her son.

Another reason she needed to work was born out of a financial arrangement that she and Jeremy had worked out with each other. In her husband's mind, Nancy was responsible for herself, and that meant paying her share of the family's expenses. From the start of their marriage, she and Jeremy had, for the most part, kept their finances separate, and even after the birth of Finny, the arrangement remained very much in place.

She casually joked to friends about the agreement, in which Jeremy was responsible for the rent and she was to pick up most of the smaller household bills. Her explanation helped friends understand why she insisted on keeping the house at a cool fifty-eight degrees in the dead of winter, and why she and Jeremy served drinks to their guests in jars that had once held fruit preserves.

Friends say that Jeremy was never happier than when he was working for Justice. He saw himself as the guy on the side of the good of the public at large, working to put the bad guys away. His job was prestigious but the salary he was earning was substantially less than the going rates for attorneys in private practice. When Nancy discussed the possibility of moving out of the city to a nearby suburb

Nancy Richards Akers
at a party in
Washington, D.C.
in 1997.
ALLAN GACKSTETTER

The house that Nancy and Jeremy once shared at 4632 Reservoir Road.

The Vietnam War Memorial, "the wall," where Jeremy Akers' body was found. DOUGLAS LOVE

Nancy and Jeremy Akers attend a black tie affair in Washington, D.C.

Jeremy Akers with close friend Bill Ranger.
ALLAN GACKSTETTER

The apartment building at 4840 MacArthur Boulevard where Nancy shared a basement apartment with her young lover, James Lemke.

U.S. Park Police Sergeant Vincent Guadioso, standing in front of police headquarters. Sergeant Guadioso discovered the body of Jeremy Akers near the Vietnam War Memorial.

LISA PULITZER

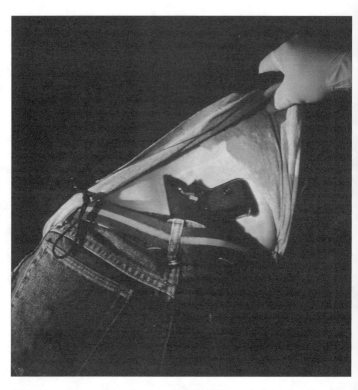

Police found the gun that Jeremy used to kill Nancy holstered to his waist.
METROPOLITAN POLICE DEPARTMENT

with more affordable rents, Jeremy turned up his nose. He did not want to have to battle the traffic to work each day, and he told his wife that he preferred to live close enough to his job that he could walk to the office.

The two agreed on a stately red-brick detached house with gracious Ionic columns on Reservoir Road, just outside of Georgetown in the fashionable Palisades/Foxhall neighborhood. Their new residence was not far from their townhouse on 44th Street.

The home's more expensive rent, and the reality that Finny was ready to start school made it clear that Nancy needed to find employment. She had already been informed that her husband did not approve of her gaining full-time employment outside the house, so she looked into the possible careers she could pursue from her home.

Short on money, and searching for a way to supplement the family's income, Nancy invited her old college roommate, Barbara Livingston, to live with them for a reasonable rent. The arrangement afforded Barbara with a decent place to stay, and the extra income that Nancy's friend was contributing each month helped her and Jeremy to meet their monthly bills.

It was sometime in 1983 that Nancy first had the idea to try her hand at romance writing. Her decision to leave the political arena, where she had worked first as a speechwriter, and later as a writer of political advertising campaigns for a prominent agency, came one afternoon during a conversation with her young son. Inquisitive little Finny never seemed to run out of questions for his mother. But the one he asked on this day sparked a fire under her. Turning to Nancy, the cherubic boy with the thick locks of curly brown hair asked, "Mommy, what are you going to be when you grow up?"

Taken aback by her young son's question, Nancy began

to revisit her past career choices, and realized that she had not felt fulfilled by her decisions. At thirty-two years old, she had spent the bulk of her career writing speeches for political candidates, and then spinning clever ad copy for the clients of the Washington advertising agency. Suddenly, she felt as though her previous contributions had made little impact on the world, and decided she wanted to pursue something more meaningful.

As Nancy began rethinking her options, her friend and housemate, Barbara Livingston, was also contemplating a career change. The reed-thin woman, working out of the small bedroom on the first floor of Nancy's home, had been engaged in a very strange profession—turning a profit by arranging the mating of Thoroughbred racehorses. While she made plenty of money, it wasn't a life choice she placed much value on. For weeks, Nancy and Barbara brainstormed, both agreeing that they wanted to make barrelfuls of money while working in the comforts of home.

For Nancy, the latter was most important, not only because she had a young boy at home, but also because her husband had made it clear that he did not want his wife working in an office setting. Realizing that her talents lay in her ability to write, Nancy suggested to Barbara that they attend a lecture to be given by a published romance writer at the local library.

Kathleen Gilles Seidel's enthusiastic presentation impressed both women. Wasting no time, Nancy raced to the phone book and called the author at her house to invite her to lunch.

"Barbara and I want to get to know you better," Nancy told Kathy. She explained that she and her friend were interested in writing romances and had been wowed by her talk earlier that week at the library.

Surprised and flattered by the solicitation, and intrigued

by Nancy and Barbara's sincere interest in her and her work, the young woman from Lawrence, Kansas, agreed to dine with them at a restaurant near her home, which was located across the Chain Bridge in neighboring Virginia.

Over overstuffed sandwiches and oversized salads, Nancy and Barbara regaled Kathy with stories of their own lives. Kathy found both women warm and funny, but Nancy especially intrigued her. The pretty woman with the crazy mane of curly dark hair was dramatic and entertaining, with a wit that was clearly gleaned from a fine education and a solid knowledge of literature. Kathy was puzzled by the disparity between Nancy's off-beat style of dress and her brilliant conversation and impeccable table manners.

She observed that the constant clicking of the dozen or so silver bracelets that encircled Nancy's wrists, and the boat-necked stretchy black shift, cut so widely that it kept slipping down her shoulder, were in stark contrast to her almost ballerina-like poise and astonishingly literate conversation. To Kathy, Nancy Richards Akers conjured up images of the character played by actress Jennifer Beals in the 1983 film, *Flashdance*—a role in which the gorgeous brunette depicted a female steel worker in masculine gear who earned extra cash at night by letting down her long locks of curly hair and moonlighting as an exotic dancer in a Pittsburgh club.

Yet, what really mystified Kathy was the formal "Thank you" card she received from Nancy several days after their lunch date even though it was Nancy who had treated her. It was handwritten in perfect penmanship on elegant stationary that was embossed with the name Mrs. Jeremy Akers. Kathy recognized that she was witnessing the kind of formal protocol used only by those of the highest pedigree.

Fortunately for Nancy, and for Barbara, Kathy was president of the newly formed Washington Romance Writers, one of just four local chapters of the Romance Writers of America. She had published her first book in 1982, and was currently launching titles for the Harlequin romance series.

During their lunch, Kathy had told Nancy that she had chosen to write romances, in part, because they were what she had always daydreamed about. As a child, the attractive Midwestern girl had spent much of her time spinning fantastical tales of love and romance. In her teenage years, she gobbled up every romance book she could find. She admired the authors of the books she read, and felt that the most important thing a person could do in a lifetime was to write a book. Even as a graduate student at a prominent East Coast university, she continued to read romances in her free hours.

As she neared the end of her academic career at Johns Hopkins University, however, she began to worry about the idea of making teaching a full-time profession. Something inside kept telling her "No." As she penned her dissertation for her Ph.D., the dreamy scenarios of her youth continued to fill her thoughts. What she finally realized was that her fantasies and the characters she so effortlessly imagined could actually be plots for books, so she secretly began putting her stories down on paper.

Determined to sell her story, Kathy packaged up her first manuscript, and sent it off to a New York publishing house. She reported proudly that in only six days, without agent representation, her submission was accepted.

Nancy found the tale enthralling. She was particularly interested in Kathy's comment that her success prompted her and other local authors to organize a local chapter of the Romance Writers of America. Nancy paid close attention as she explained that the idea for the regional organization was to provide a way for writers to network, and a place for them to sit and exchange ideas, and that another goal was to help aspiring authors like Nancy and Barbara get published.

For Nancy, membership made perfect sense. Like Kathy, she loved romances, and had been reading them voraciously since her early teens. She wanted to use her talents as a writer, and was very interested in the financial aspect of the business, as she desperately needed to earn a living.

From the very first meeting, Nancy threw herself into the organization. She immediately introduced herself to the thirty or so people in attendance, among them such rising stars as Nora Roberts and Diane Chamberlain. Hoping to learn from the roomful of literati, Nancy chatted with as many of the members as she could. Over time, she learned that many of them had children at home, and like her, were looking for an outlet in which they could utilize their writing talents, earn a decent living, and still be home for their little ones.

One of the first members Nancy befriended was Kathleen Karr. The petite redhead with the wire-rimmed glasses had found WRW through an announcement in the local paper touting the newly formed organization as a group of professional romance writers able to help aspiring authors to get published.

Like Nancy, Kathleen had a background in English. Having completed a degree at Catholic University in Washington, DC, she had followed her husband, a fellow student, to Brown University, where he enrolled in a Ph.D. program in theoretical physics. Both Kathleen and her husband loved film, and spent all of their spare time working for the National Endowment for the Arts in Rhode Island. There, they helped set up the first state-run film archive in the country. The pilot project was so successful that it was used as a model for other states. When the couple completed their studies in Rhode Island, they were both offered positions with the American Film Institute in Washington. Excitedly, they packed up their belongings and headed to the Capital City. When they arrived, they purchased an old, dilapidated townhouse in an up-and-coming area of town, and spent the next few years restoring it to its original glory.

Kathleen left her post with the AFI after one year and took a part-time job running a group of motion picture houses. The Old Circle Theater Group was considered the best repertory house in the country, and she was at the helm. Standing barely five feet tall, the intelligent young writer had just given birth to her second child. Both she and her husband were avid readers and spent most of their evenings snuggled in bed with their heads in a book. But Kathleen was growing increasingly frustrated with the quality of the novels she was reading. Night after night, she would toss the books on the floor and announce that she could write better herself.

"So, why don't you?" her husband challenged her.

"Okay, I will," she responded with an air of confidence.

She continued her part-time work with the Old Circle Theater Group, and in her spare time, worked on what she hoped would be a saleable manuscript. Kathleen had written two complete books—neither of them publishable—when she opened the newspaper to find the blurb announcing the meeting of the WRW. "There is somebody else out there trying to do what I am trying to do!" she exclaimed. She felt her heart beating with excitement as she dialed the number for more information.

But her excitement was tempered by the response she got from the woman on the other end of the receiver. At first, the voice had seemed encouraging.

"Please come," the woman urged Kathy, and graciously invited her to the upcoming meeting.

"I must bring my baby," Kathleen announced, explaining that her son was just a few months old and that she was still nursing.

"I'm sorry, no babies allowed," the woman answered sternly. "This is a professional organization, and we don't talk about our children or our families here. This is about your writing career. We talk about how to be a better writer, and how to get published."

Kathleen was taken aback by the woman's pointed response, but at the same time, she was desperate to succeed as a writer. She arranged for her husband to watch her infant son and reluctantly went off to the meeting. When she arrived, she learned that the WRW had only been in existence for eight months, but had already attracted an impressive group of talented young authors.

For Kathleen, the WRW turned out to be tremendously supportive, and its rules could not have been more suited to her purpose. Most of the thirty or so women were juggling full-time jobs and children, and relished the idea of getting together once a month to talk about what was really a passion for them. They considered the organization their university and the seminars were tailored to meet their individual needs. The meetings were totally focused on a manuscript that a publishing house would find worthy of optioning. Little else was mentioned during the rigorous Saturday morning sessions.

Like Kathleen, many of the women had chosen to pursue a career in romance writing because it allowed them to expand on their own fantasies, and held greater promise of publication than did children's books or science fiction, in which developing a following could take up to ten years. Romance writing—when successful—allowed new authors to get noticed quickly.

This was Nancy's hope. She was certain that with her

background in literature and English, and her years as a professional writer, she would be able to bang out a compelling romance book with ease. What she and Barbara discovered, however, was that writing a seventy- to one-hundred-thousand-word manuscript with a good plot and decent dialogue was an arduous chore, and that it wasn't as easy as they thought to get published. For months, Nancy and her collaborator diligently attended the Saturday meetings that were often held in the auditoriums of the theaters that Kathleen Karr represented.

Published authors such as Kathy Seidel and Nora Roberts, who were both members of the group, gave seminars on various aspects of writing, providing instruction on how to improve dialogue and tips on how to get published. Agents and editors from New York City also took the hour-long plane ride to Washington to teach members how to target their work toward the publishing houses that were most likely to be interested.

At first, Nancy and Barbara collaborated, choosing to focus on short, contemporary romance because, they learned, the slim volumes promised the greatest financial reward. For months, the women wrote and rewrote scenario after scenario, but in spite of their efforts and the coaching they received from members of the WRW, they were unsuccessful. Later that year, Barbara packed up her things and moved out of state, leaving Nancy determined to succeed on her own.

Nancy had grown fond of the women of the WRW, and found the environment both nurturing and supportive. Its members provided a lot of positive energy and encouraging feedback, and the monthly work sessions enabled her to escape her harried life and concentrate solely on writing. As it turned out, Kathleen Karr lived not far from Nancy and Jeremy. Kathleen's older child, Suzanne, was the same age as Finny, and the two children were enrolled at the same private school. Sometimes they would arrange to get together and talk about their work, while Finny and Suzanne played in Kathleen's basement.

On many mornings, Kathleen stopped in on Nancy on her way back from dropping off her daughter at the prestigious St. Patrick's Episcopal Day School. She was always impressed to find her friend seated in her first-floor office, clad in a bathrobe and slippers, and sipping from the oversized cup of coffee she kept beside her on the desk.

Kathleen knew all too well that the life of a writer was one of isolation and that sitting for hours at the typewriter, laboring over every word and turn of phrase could be both frustrating and discouraging. Yet, there was something oddly thrilling about hovering at the keyboard in pajamas for much of the day, slurping down cup after cup of coffee while spinning tales of love. Neither woman could think of anything else they would rather do, and both were convinced they would surely succeed.

Kathleen knew from her visits to Nancy's place that her friend had a penchant for amusing pieces of furniture and whimsical artifacts. In the center of her living room, which was decorated in bold colors and showy prints, she kept a pair of huge, ornate birdcages inhabited by the birds that her husband had purchased when the family lived in Florida. On some afternoons she opened the tiny wire doors to let her feathered friends spread their wings. Nancy could not stop raving about the antique dressmaker's form that she had found tucked away in a corner of Kathleen's basement. She fell in love with the wiry figure and was thrilled when Kathleen gave it to her as a special gift from friend to friend.

Kathleen could not help but smile each time she stopped by for a chat and saw the way Nancy had dressed the figure, which she proudly displayed at the entranceway of her ornately decorated home. It amazed and amused her that nearly every week, Nancy would change the mannequin's attire, clothing it in everything from fancy dresses to glitzy boas. Her friends didn't find Nancy's interest in costuming the wiry figure at all unusual since she did everything with style and flair, outfitting herself in vivid, prismatic clothes, and embracing an exotic collection of family pets that included snakes, a macaw, a parrot, a ferret, and a spindly old cat.

It did not take long for Kathleen to benefit from her affiliation with the WRW. After only six months, she was ecstatic to learn that her third manuscript had been accepted for publication. Bursting to share her good news, she jumped into her car and raced over to Nancy's house, finding her, as usual, seated in her first-floor office, wrapped in a robe that barely concealed her frilly nightgown. Barely able to contain her excitement, Kathleen blurted out the details of her publishing arrangement as the two women jumped up and down and squealed with delight. Word that Kathleen had successfully placed her book was genuinely thrilling to Nancy, and it made her believe even more that she would be next. With renewed optimism, the determined young mother continued to write.

By the spring of 1984, Nancy had not yet found the recipe for a successful manuscript. As much as she struggled to conjure a winning formula for short contemporary romances, she was finding it impossible to find the voice that love stories set in the twentieth century require.

She did, however, change the way in which the women of the WRW hosted their meetings. Before Nancy joined the group, the members served coffee in white Styrofoam cups and set out cake and pastries on paper plates. Forever the gracious host, Nancy insisted they make a change.

When the vivacious Junior Leaguer learned that the WRW was planning an event at Kathy Seidel's house in nearby Virginia, she quickly offered her help. "Ladies," Nancy informed the meeting, playfully affecting a King's English accent, "we simply *must* use china." When she arrived at Kathy's front door, she held a large wicker basket with enough crockery to stock a small specialty shop. Delicate porcelain cups and saucers, arranged tastefully alongside cloth napkins and tablecloths, had been packed with care.

As she stepped into the foyer, the spirited brunette in the colorful print dress threw back her locks of long, curly hair with dramatic flair, and with a wave of her hand announced in the perfect tones of an upper-class Brahmin: "We don't *have* to use the china, but why not?" Without missing a beat—and to the delighted giggles of Kathy and the other members—she transformed herself effortlessly into a Cockney-accented Eliza Doolittle, making it clear that she had not only brought fine china to the occasion but also that she was completely prepared to peddle a pocketful of posies.

As the women continued to ooh and aah at Nancy's performance, the former thespian arranged the food carefully on the fancy platters that she had lined with doilies, garnishing each one with a sprig of parsley and slices of fresh fruit. They were spellbound by the way she tended the dishes, making certain that each plate was freshened and re-garnished whenever needed.

Having grown up in a small college town in Kansas, Kathy had never seen such a presentation. Over the years, her mother had entertained countless guests in their Lawrence home, but not once with such pomp and circumstance. For Kathy, Nancy embodied the Martha Stewart touch, years before the home décor queen had become famous. It was a manner that, from that day forward, Kathy and many of the other members would emulate. Nancy had opened their eyes to a world that many had only read about, and they agreed to employ her opulent entertaining style at all of their big events.

But while Nancy was building a reputation as an expert party-planner, her attempts at writing were not going nearly as well. Bolstered by the successes of several more members of the Washington Romance Writers, Nancy continued to struggle with her contemporary romances. Even when it was becoming apparent to her and everyone else in the group that she could not find the winning formula, she continued to dream of the financial rewards a finished and optioned book could yield. It was during one of her many conversations with author Kathy Seidel that she realized that she could not produce a publishable manuscript on a topic for which she had no passion. Yet, she resisted relinquishing her original goal and chose to persevere. Like her husband, Nancy was not one to give up without a good fight.

After several more attempts, however, Nancy finally conceded that she could not write contemporaries on her own. She concluded that her expertise was as a researcher and not a chronicler of human experience, and that her inability to draft a saleable manuscript was due to her lack of emotional maturity. She decided to heed Kathy Seidel's advice that she switch to Regencies.

Traditional Regencies are smaller books, usually around 200 pages, that contain very little sex. They are set in England during the Regency period, which spanned 1811–1820, when blind, insane George III was king, but the Prince Regent was the *de facto* ruler. The books focus on the details of the period, rather than the intricacies of a tempestuous love affair between a man and a woman.

Nancy's party-throwing talents, and the ease with which she catered the small gathering at Kathy's house, paled in comparison to the feat she would accomplish next. Drawing on her extensive experience working with not-for-profit corporations, she put her unmatchable organizational skills to work to coordinate the first romance-writers' retreat. Her idea for the weekend conference was to provide writers with a refuge where they could learn from key players in the publishing industry, and, at the same time, be inspired by the tranquility of a getaway in a beautiful country setting.

Nancy was a *very* political person, constantly aware of the dynamics of a group, whether it was the Junior League or the United States of America. She believed that having just one editor and one agent on hand to give advice and critique members' work would be more helpful than a roomful of lecturers and a schedule that demanded attending countless workshops.

The two-day event was planned for the Hilltop House Hotel and Conference Center in the tiny Civil War town of Harpers Ferry, West Virginia. Built at the turn of the century, the lovely four-story, brick-and-wood Hilltop House sat perched high atop a cliff in the majestic Blue Ridge Mountains, affording guests spectacular views of the junction of the Shenandoah and Potomac Rivers and an ambience of serenity. The adjacent small town of vertical streets lined with cafes, antique shops, pottery and craft stores, and an authentic wax museum, made it the perfect site for the weekend respite that Nancy had in mind. She especially liked that members could hike along the river and enjoy fishing, boating, and picnicking in nearby Harpers Ferry National Historical Park. Sightseers could also climb a steep alpine trail to a small cemetery, where, standing amid the graves, they could take in the sweeping view of West

Virginia, Maryland, and Virginia. The women especially delighted in a story told to them by members of the hotel staff. They heard that in an amusing turn of events, the town had undergone a permanent name change probably around 1910, or more specifically a permanent name-spelling change. The apostrophe before the "s" in the word *Harper's* was forever dropped after the painter who was commissioned by the town to design the official sign accidentally left it out. Unwilling to spend the additional money to have the marker repainted, the town council voted to eliminate the apostrophe forever. The story which could not be verified by local historians, was not lost on the women, who took every facet of the English language seriously.

When members arrived in April of 1985 for the first annual Romance Writers Retreat the breathtaking scenery overwhelmed them. The crabapple and cherry trees were in full blossom, and brilliant yellow daffodils covered the rolling green hills surrounding the decades-old hotel. The site had been chosen by Anita Brown, the director of the conference center and a part owner. She had negotiated an enticingly low weekend package rate for the women of WRW, of which she was a member.

While everyone agreed that the setting was lovely and even more than most could have dreamed of, the accommodations had some members complaining. The hotel had fallen into a state of disrepair, with sinks hanging crookedly from the walls in the bathroom, the hot water running out before they finished their showers, and the wallpaper peeling off the walls. And there were no telephones in the rooms!

But for the most part, the women disregarded the somewhat seedy accommodations and delighted instead in the bucolic setting, and the program that had been planned for them by Nancy. They were aware that Nancy's idea for the weekend was to provide them with a *true* retreat atmosphere. And they appreciated that, unlike most writers' conferences, the workshops would feature only one editor and one agent, speaking directly to their needs. They weren't disappointed. The workshops were of an academic, almost scholarly, nature, with only a handful devoted to the current status of the romance market.

For Nancy and the others, it was an opportunity to learn first-hand from important people in the industry, and a chance to laugh, sip wine, and tell stories at impromptu pajama parties that snowballed in the hotel rooms of the WRW members. Many of the women had already forged friendships during the Saturday sessions, but much of their conversation had been focused solely on their professional goals. Being away for an entire weekend afforded them time to talk on a more personal level.

But Nancy was not one to mix her private and professional life, and did not share a lot in the way of personal information. Most of the women knew very little about her background, and even less about her husband. When the meetings were held at her home on Reservoir Road, members would catch little more than a glimpse and a grin from Nancy's craggy, blonde-haired, blue-eyed spouse.

One woman in particular had a negative image of Nancy's relationship with Jeremy. Kathy Seidel frequently got together with Nancy to discuss their careers. However, their conversation often digressed into more personal topics, becoming a chance to air typical complaints about married life. The two women found it a relief to complain to each other about their husbands' failure to participate in the household chores, and to commiserate about how much more they could get done when the men were not underfoot. Kathy's impression was that her friend's husband was "controlling and prickly." She was therefore surprised by Nancy's report of Jeremy's response to her homecoming at the end of the retreat weekend.

She listened in amazement as Nancy related the details of the romantic evening her husband had planned for her upon her return. Jeremy told his wife just how glad he was that she was home by drawing her a hot bubble bath in a darkened room illuminated only by candles, then serving her a glass of wine as she luxuriated in the steamy tub. Nancy used the word "caretaking" to describe her husband's welcoming gesture, surprising her with the realization that there was another side to the Akerses' marriage.

Making a calculated change of paths was sobering. While Nancy had heard the earning potential on contemporaries was unlimited, even reaching six figures, Regencies had a definite ceiling. But Nancy's main concern was getting published—no matter what the financial rewards.

Around the time that Nancy decided to try a different tack, she learned that an author of several published contemporaries named Mary Kilchenstein had joined the Washington Romance Writers. She was thrilled when the successful writer telephoned her to say she would be attending the Writers Retreat at Harpers Ferry in April that Nancy had dreamed up and decided to organize. While they had spoken briefly over the phone, discussing Mary's room reservation at the Hilltop House, she could hardly wait to meet her in person. She knew that Mary, who was writing under the name *Jean Fauré,* had had success writing contemporary romance. Nancy was desperate to learn her secrets.

For Nancy, the high point of the retreat was meeting Mary Kilchenstein. Upon arriving in West Virginia, Nancy immediately introduced herself to the tall, woman with the straight brown hair, who was pretty in an understated way. She began plying her with questions about her burgeoning writing career. The course of the conversation revealed that Nancy and Mary shared many of the same interests. Both women had enjoyed a musical childhood, with Nancy studying dance and Mary the piano. Nancy had majored in international relations in college, while Mary held a degree in American studies.

Nancy listened attentively as Mary explained that her older son, Peter, was four and a half years old and she had been pregnant with her second son, David, when she sold her first book in February of 1984. *Bed of Roses* was released under the name *Jean Fauré* and was published by Second Chance at Love, a Berkley imprint that several years later would be discontinued. The two women talked about Mary's most recent works, which included several contemporaries and an historical. As the evening wore on, Nancy asked to take a look at some of Mary's writings. Flattered by her acquaintance's interest, Mary went to her hotel room and pulled out a few manuscripts she had written that had not yet been published, and gave them to Nancy to take home.

Several days later, Mary received a telephone call from her newest fan. Nancy lauded Mary's ability to develop a plot and liked the way she effected characterization. As the two women chatted about the various scenarios Mary had written, Nancy boldly confessed that she had all but given up on writing contemporaries. She explained that she had worked for nearly two years with no success, and admitted that she believed the reason was that she lacked the kind of insight necessary to be successful in the lucrative genre.

To Mary's surprise, Nancy revealed that, after much contemplation, she had concluded that her inability to succeed was directly linked to her own emotional immaturity.

She told Mary that she thought of herself as an emotional adolescent, and worried that her naiveté was what was hindering her chances for success. Then she suggested something that caught Mary completely off guard. Nancy proposed that they work together on a manuscript—hoping that collaboration with Mary would provide her with an opportunity to learn from an accomplished pro.

Astonished by the offer, and flattered by Nancy's honesty and praise, Mary agreed to work with the bold and seemingly capable woman. Pulling four or five synopses from her files, she presented them to Nancy at their next meeting. She explained that they were various stories that she was considering developing, and advised Nancy to take them home and look them over, and then choose one that struck her fancy.

Excitedly, Nancy reviewed the outlines and then called her new mentor to say she had found a storyline that had captured her imagination. The two women agreed to meet and hold a plotting session. They spent hours sitting together in Mary's backyard in Rockville, Maryland, exchanging ideas and acting out a variety of scenarios. Every so often, they would take a break to speak about the flowers in Mary's garden and to check on Peter, Mary's eldest son, and Finny playing together on the swing set that Mary and her husband had set up on the lawn.

Once Nancy and Mary had decided upon a scenario to their mutual liking, they agreed to divide the work: Nancy as researcher, Mary as writer. The women spoke almost every day, with Mary calling in to advise Nancy of her progress and Nancy helping to fill in any holes that she noticed as she reviewed the drafts. But with little involvement in the actual writing of the book, Nancy continued to work on her own manuscript, a Regency romance entitled *The Mayfair Season*. She had advised Mary that she planned to continue her efforts, and was pleased when Mary agreed that it would not interfere with their collaboration.

The story that Nancy was concocting was set in 1816. It was the tale of Miss Mina O'Keiffe of Thornhill Park, Kent, a seventeen-year-old maiden who was eleven years old when her mother, Lady Elaine, died. She was then forced to live with her quick-tempered older brothers in a rambling Tudor manor house in the English countryside.

"In her innocence, Mina did not realize that she had been welcomed into Society merely out of sympathy for her mother," Nancy wrote. "Mama, gay and beautiful, had been the only child of the Marquess of Thornbury, a thoroughly dissolute nobleman, who, having gambled away the family fortune, bartered his daughter to a wealthy Irish merchant."

The story contained remarkable similarities to Nancy's own life, in which she grew up a modern-day maiden with two petulant brothers and a society mother in a Tudor manor home. Even Miss Mina's love interest, Lord Compton Cavendish, the Seventh Earl of Brierly, with his fair hair, sky-blue eyes, and cool, detached attitude toward love and everlasting relationships, resembled Nancy's own husband.

With two years of writing under her belt, Nancy was determined to make this book her big sale, and as her collaboration with Mary progressed, she paid close attention to her co-author's style, especially the way she developed the plot and fleshed out the characters. Mary understood Nancy's determination and provided her with help whenever she asked. She was aware that many authors spend much more than two years honing their craft and collecting rejections, and encouraged Nancy to persevere. Mary was impressed by her new associate's playful sense of humor, and believed that Nancy's natural flair for storytelling, and her literary ability to paint vivid images that described events and places like no one she had ever known, would ultimately land her a publishing contract.

Yet while Mary liked Nancy personally, she was keenly aware that her new writing partner was accustomed to a lifestyle that was very different from her own. Nancy did little to hide the fact that she had been raised in an upper-crust world, but while she routinely dropped names of the important people she knew, she also poked fun at the aristocratic people she had grown up with. After attending a breakfast meeting of one of her society clubs, she jokingly employed a wide range of hilarious voices as she described the expensive alligator shoes and lengthy false eyelashes that were flaunted by the women in attendance. That they found it necessary to dress to the nines so early each morning was endlessly amusing to Nancy.

When the plotting sessions were held at Nancy's home, Mary noted that the residence was accented with expensive, hand-enameled Cloisonné eggs, distinctive blue-and-white Spode china, and fancy snuff boxes that her family had purchased over the years at Sotheby's auctions. The glass etageres in her colorful living room showcased a collection of fine bric-a-brac items that were clearly worth hundreds and even thousands of dollars.

For Nancy, holidays—especially Christmas—offered the opportunity to celebrate in grand style, and her friends marveled at her elaborate preparations. Just days before Christmas Eve, the aspiring author waved her husband and son farewell as they jaunted off to the country to cut down a fifteen-foot white pine and cart it back to Washington, where it was elaborately bedecked with fanciful ornaments and sparkling tinsel, and proudly displayed in the family's well-appointed dining room. When she couldn't bear to part with the fragrant tree, she redecorated it with crimson hearts that she had cut out by hand in honor of St. Valentine's

Day. Another aspect of holiday celebrations was the opportunity to showcase the expensive silverware she had inherited from her grandparents, a family heirloom of which she was particularly proud.

But the contradictions in her relationship to possessions and formality remained, extending far beyond holiday celebrations. While she counted membership at a yacht club on the Long Island Sound among her many childhood affiliations, and often chatted about her ongoing association with the Junior League, she continued to serve her guests drinks out of the recycled jelly jars.

Despite the great amount of valuable appointments, the overall impression given by Nancy's home was one of complete chaos. Several of the couple's friends described the Akers residence as "a wreck." Every surface was cluttered, not only with fine *objets d'art* but also with papers, date books, clothing, toys, and the artifacts of everyday life. According to those close to Nancy, Jeremy was the culprit. While Nancy viewed his frequent absences as an opportunity to restore order in the house, upon his return he would immediately create disarray. He would dump his legal papers on the dining room table, then go into the kitchen and pull a box of his favorite cereal and a can of the coffee he drank every morning out of the cabinet, insisting they be kept on the compact kitchen counter for his own convenience. Jeremy's friends told a different tale. They claimed that Nancy was "no housekeeper" and that Jeremy often complained about the state of their home. At any rate, money was short in the Akers household, and Nancy's attempts to juggle the raising of her children with the fulfillment of her aspirations left little time for the non-stop demands of housekeeping.

For a while, Nancy employed a homeless person she had rescued from the streets to help with some of the housework, an African American man she had met through Grate Patrol, an organization Nancy had found time to initiate with Katherine Karr, to feed the city's homeless. Through her work as a member of the Junior League of Washington, Nancy had become especially sensitive to the plight of those less fortunate than she. As a mother, she was interested in teaching Finny and the other students attending St. Patrick's Episcopal Day School about the importance of helping others. Her idea was to bring food to the city's homeless and encourage the young students to distribute the brown-bag meals of sandwiches and juice on their weekly trips to the areas in the inner city where the homeless slept. Not only did the children hand out the lunches; they also participated in preparing and packaging the meals, meeting at Nancy's or Kathy's house in the early morning to ready them for delivery.

The street people were so receptive to the children that they remained sober and clean in anticipation of their arrival. When the volunteers' special van pulled up to the curb, they greeted the children warmly, sometimes regaling them with their woeful stories and always admonishing them to stay away from drugs and alcohol. The volunteer efforts continued year-round, but were especially appreciated on the holidays.

Money, or the lack of it, her friend Mary would learn, was a major theme in Nancy's life and the most powerful motivation to becoming a published author. They often ate at local pizza parlors, and not the expensive restaurants of Nancy's youth. Mary often wondered if Nancy's house was so cold in wintertime, and so dimly lit, to cut down on utility bills. She knew the Akerses were very environmentally conscious, counting membership in organizations such as the Chesapeake Bay Fund among their affiliations. But she suspected that the frigid indoor climate had less to do with the ideology and more to do with saving pennies.

While her collaborator was not one for intimate, self-disclosing talk, Mary did pick up dribs and drabs about her friend's early life as a child of privilege in Scarsdale. During their plotting sessions, Mary listened attentively when Nancy opened up with brief remembrances from her childhood and the problematic relationship that she had had with her mother. She learned that Roderick and Susan Richards had generously agreed to help their daughter with Finny's private school tuition, but that their involvement with Nancy and her husband had diminished over the years. By the time the two women began to collaborate on writing projects, Nancy was barely speaking to her mother. Even visits from her oldest brother, with whom she had been very close during childhood, seemed to stir up anxiety in Nancy.

Although many of the problems that existed between Nancy and her mother stemmed from things that occurred during Nancy's childhood years, their already strained relationship worsened after Nancy's marriage to Jeremy.

Nancy did not speak much of her husband to her friend, but it was clear to Mary that she preferred not having him around. It was almost as if he got in her way, making irritating demands and interrupting her normal routine. On the rare occasions that Jeremy was at home during their writing sessions, he poked his head in to say a fast hello before disappearing to another part of the house. Mary sensed this enormous energy emanating from the forty-something man with the rugged good looks. She found his deep, resonant voice and Southern accent seductive, and noticed that in addition to his manly physique and chiseled features, he had a very forceful presence that made it almost impossible to look away from him when he entered the tiny first-floor office. Yet while he was always courtly and polite, there was something unsettling about Jeremy that stirred concern in Mary.

In a very short time, Nancy and Mary accomplished much more than simply developing a warm friendship. Remarkably, their combined energy led to the completion of their first manuscript in just three weeks. Both women were comfortable with the arrangement they agreed upon at the beginning of the collaboration, that Nancy's contribution would be less than Mary's. While both women participated in plotting the book, Nancy's only other role was doing sporadic research and writing short sections to fill in the gaps, primarily descriptions of setting, which were Nancy's real strength.

Mary, meanwhile, actually wrote the entire manuscript. Although they both held the copyright, *In Your Wildest Dreams* was published under a pseudonym, *Mary Alice Kirk*. The two women even created a biography for the "author," combining bits and pieces of both their backgrounds.

Silhouette Books released the novel, which was just short of two hundred pages, in November of 1987. The story involved two single parents, Caroline Forrester, an attractive young health-education teacher and mother of a teen-aged boy, and Greg Lawton, the handsome father of a teen-aged girl, who becomes outraged about the sex-education "lessons" his daughter is learning in Caroline's classroom. When Greg storms into school to protest, the attraction between him and Caroline is immediate and powerful. Soon, the two learn their own lessons about romance and love.

Rather than dedicating the book to their own love interests, Nancy and Mary dedicated *In Your Wildest Dreams* to their sons:

To Peter, Finny and David, beloved eggs, who with paper airplanes, buckets of crayfish, flies taped to windowpanes, and enough messy diapers to single-handedly keep Pampers in business, make life so very interesting.

While the book's publication was exciting, its production had been severely delayed. In addition, it was greatly overshadowed by an even more dramatic success: the publication of the first book that Nancy wrote alone. *The Mayfair Season*, released under the name Nancy Richards Akers, and written during her collaboration with Mary, was sold to Warner Books and debuted the same year. Despite the oddly coincidental timing of the books' publication, 1987 marked the fulfillment of Nancy's dreams. To show her appreciation to those who had helped her along the way, she wrote the following dedication:

To the memory of my grandfather, John Rehm, with my love. And in gratitude to Pam Regis, Kath Seidel, Myra Engers, Barbara Livingston, Diann Litvin, and Mary Kilchenstein, with my thanks.

Immediately after the manuscript for *In Your Wildest Dreams* was completed, the two women got to work on another collaboration. Their second book was the story of a ten-year relationship between Laurel and Nathan, who marry despite a built-in conflict: Nathan's insistence upon pursuing a career in the military that prevents Laurel from setting down roots and having the family of her dreams. The heroine's dilemma is complicated by the fact that her father was a military man, dragging her from place to place during her childhood. Ultimately, the couple's marriage ends in divorce, but the sudden death of Nathan's uncle brings them back together again. The couple goes on to heal the wounds of the past, finally reuniting in marriage.

The second collaboration between Nancy and Mary did not go as smoothly as the first. Once again the women met for plotting sessions, and together they embarked on the research. They met regularly at Mary's home in Baltimore, kicking around ideas with a tape recorder running.

In this effort, as in their first collaboration, Nancy did not participate in the actual writing of the book, although she did play a greater role in the researching of the story. Mary, in turn, checked in with Nancy often to let her know how she was progressing with the manuscript, as she was writing the book entirely on her own.

When Nancy read the finished product, she regretfully told Mary of her disappointment with the story. In between apologies, she explained that she found the book boring. Hearing that her writing partner was dissatisfied with her work devastated Mary, who was inwardly quite emotional and sensitive. But the fact that Nancy kept apologizing allowed Mary not to take the criticism to heart. Obligingly she began a second draft. But when Nancy announced that she hated the second version as well, Mary grew impatient. She went through the manuscript page by page, studying the markings Nancy had made. She was astounded to find that Nancy had discarded every section in which one of the characters was experiencing internal machinations, wrestling with emotional conflicts in the way most troubled people do.

Uncertain of how to interpret Nancy's criticism, Mary sent the manuscript off to both the editor and the agent representing the two authors. They both loved it. Mary was relieved, but not really surprised that the publishing professionals confirmed what she already knew, that the backbone of a romance novel is the development of a relationship between the hero and the heroine, and the climax is the resolution of the conflict that persists in keeping them apart.

The finished product, minus Nancy's suggested changes, was entitled *Promises* and released in 1988 as a Silhouette Special Edition paperback. The series featured other realistic stories of intense romance. Although Nancy remained unhappy with the book, her name still appeared on the copyright. But at her own suggestion, the two did not split the royalties 60–40 the way they had on their first collaboration. Instead, Nancy settled for considerably less.

Besides, Nancy had two major preoccupations of her own. One was the release and publication of *The Mayfair Season*. The second was much more personal: learning that she was pregnant with her second child.

For years, she had been talking about her desire to have another child, and was beginning to lose hope when she learned that she would become a mother for a second time. Being a parent to a house full of children had always been Nancy's greatest desire. She had once confided to Mary how sorry she was that she had not been able to increase the size of her family. Nancy's hopes were shared by her son, Finny, who had religiously asked his parents for a baby brother or sister every Christmas since he was able to speak.

While Nancy's career as a writer had certainly had its ups and downs, her success with motherhood had never been less than stellar. She treasured her times with Finny, and was constantly creating innovative methods to broaden his perspective and educate him about the world. She read him sophisticated stories as a way of expanding his experience, and after they moved to Washington, took him on regular visits to the museums lining the city's famous mall.

For fun, every Halloween Nancy designed elaborate costumes for her and her son, sewing together a variety of fabrics to which she glued glitter and beads. Excitedly, she created characters for Finny, and then patterned ghoulish outfits—witches and goblins—that she wore to the delight of her son and his young friends. Her face painted with theatrical makeup, she accompanied the children as they rang doorbells and shouted, "Trick or Treat!"

News that Nancy was pregnant had Finny ecstatic, and he excitedly counted the days until he could meet and play with his new sibling. But his mother's pregnancy was troublesome. Her entire body swelled from all the water she was retaining, and she gained more than seventy pounds. For a woman as concerned with her appearance as she had always been, the ballooning reflection in the mirror was devastating to her. Keeping up with her regular schedule of mothering and writing became increasingly difficult.

On April 5, 1988, Nancy gave birth to Saier William Zeb Davis Akers. The birth of her second boy was as traumatic as the pregnancy, with the long, difficult labor ending in a C-section. In selecting a name for their new son, Nancy and Jeremy followed the same path they had chosen when they had named Finny: using the names of the Confederate colonels and generals among Jeremy's family members and people he admired who had fought against the Union in the Civil War.

Adding a new baby to the mix meant added expenses for the family, and less time for Nancy to work on her manuscripts. The advance she and Mary had received for *Promises* had been barely enough to cover the cost of her family's food and electric bills. The total advance and royalties for the two collaborations was in the area of $32,000 including royalties earned over several years. With a monthly rental payment in excess of $2,000, coupled with household expenses and Finny's private school, even the monies she received from *The Mayfair Season* and her second Regency, *A Season Abroad*, also released in 1988, did not boost Nancy's income to a satisfactory level.

Her husband's announcement the following year that he had been offered a new, higher-paying job could not have been better timed. Jeremy suddenly had an opportunity to work as an executive for a private international company that provided environmental consulting services to U.S. and foreign corporations. The offer meant a significant increase from his current government salary as well as a high profile position in the private sector.

Jeremy's new job as Director of Corporate Services for Kroll Environmental Services in Washington, DC, required traveling all over the United States. His role was to supervise investigative teams at hazardous waste sites, to reconstruct site histories, and to identify the character and source of waste contained in the site. He was also expected to oversee allocation projects at the sites in which contributing parties were assigned liability based upon their individual percentages of waste volume toxicity, and supervise witness and asset searches. His duties extended to acting as liaison between corporate clients and local and federal regulatory agencies.

Unlike his job with the Justice Department, where he spent a good deal of time in the courtroom trying cases against violators of the EPA's statutes, he was now working for the corporations he had once prosecuted, helping them to troubleshoot potential problems. As supervisor, he partook in the ongoing investigation of suspected Superfund sites with an eye to identifying all the parties who were responsible, in order to allocate the liability fairly.

In spite of his significantly larger paycheck, Jeremy still expected Nancy to contribute to the household expenses. Friends observed that whenever he got his hands on some extra money he would spend it on himself, purchasing a new kayak, exercise equipment, or some other self-indulgence. It was a responsibility that Nancy did not seem to mind, but one that she felt increasingly anxious about fulfilling, since taking care of Finny and the new baby was so demanding. But with Jeremy out of the house and on the road for much of the month, she found herself adjusting to the life of a single mother, setting her own time schedules, and managing to mother the kids, get the meals served, and continue her writing.

While she was somewhat overwhelmed, she nevertheless liked the feeling of freedom that Jeremy's travels afforded her. Able to work whenever she wanted, and clear of the responsibility of keeping the kind of neat house he liked, she could devote all of her free hours to her writing pursuits. But the balance she happily achieved in her work and her personal life was short-lived.

When Zeb was only six months old, Nancy became pregnant again. And this pregnancy was even more demanding than before. Once again, she ballooned up, gaining massive amounts of weight and severely retaining water. The pregnancy also ended in a C-section.

Grierson Isabelle Virginia Akers was born on August 10, 1989. While the period following Nancy's last pregnancy had been enjoyable, this time was extremely stressful. Experiencing two difficult pregnancies in a row had depleted her physically, and taking care of two infants and an older child virtually on her own exacted an emotional toll on Nancy.

With so much on her plate, and her husband on the road for weeks, sometimes months, at a time, she had little time to socialize with the friends she had made through the Washington Romance Writers. Yet, every so often, one of the women would hear about a calamity in Nancy's life and call or visit to lend a sympathetic ear. Kathleen Karr learned that the family Macaw had bitten off a piece of young Isabelle's finger, and Mary heard from their mutual agent, Adele Leone, that Nancy had been rushed to the hospital with some kind of systemic infection.

To help her through the ordeal, Nancy employed various high school girls to act as nannies for her children after school, and continued to use the services of the young man she had hired to clean her large house. In addition to tidying, Ulysses, the man Nancy had found through the Grate Patrol, lifted the mood of the house as he sang his way through the cleaning chores—at one point he had even earned part of his living singing songs on street corners to passers-by. Not only was he a wonderful housekeeper, he had a riotous sense of humor, and a flair for the dramatic.

But things continued to deteriorate. Soon after Isabelle's first birthday, Jeremy announced that he intended to quit his job and start his own consulting firm. As one of only a handful of people trained in his field of environmental law, he was certain that going out on his own would provide him with a greater income, and more control over his hours.

His new company, Environmental Strategies Management, was a consulting firm that combined legal, investigative, scientific, and technical know-how on a broad range of services, including responsible-party identification and asset searches, reconstruction site histories, environmental audits and assessments, cost allocations, and public-relations services. Jeremy was the company's chief executive and planned to operate out of the family's house.

Soon after Jeremy's old housemate Don Boswell heard that his friend was planning to venture out on his own, he extended him an invitation to join the law firm he founded in Palm Beach, Florida. It would be an easy move for Jeremy because he was already a member of the Florida Bar as a result of his work with the State Attorney's Office.

Jeremy accepted Don's offer, and Don added his name to the firm's letterhead. Yet, their partnership never really got off the ground. Jeremy met with Don and prospective clients during his trips to Florida, but he was so busy with his environmental consulting firm that he never seemed to have the time to give the new alliance the attention that Don had hoped.

But Don kept the partnership in place, figuring that Jeremy would eventually find the time to devote to the venture. He had remained in close contact with the Akers family since they had left Florida and moved back to Washington in 1983. He stopped in for dinner whenever he was in town on business, and kept the lines of communication open with thirty-minute conference calls between himself, Jeremy, and Nancy at least once every other month.

Jeremy stayed at Don's place whenever he was in Florida on a case, and Jeremy returned the favor with an open invitation to his family's home on Reservoir Road. Don was a confirmed bachelor, and he was accustomed to keeping his home and possessions in impeccably neat order. He found the Akers place in disarray—so much so that he had a hard time coping with spending his nights there when he was in town.

He had always found Nancy to be a lovely woman, but it was clear that she did not have time for housework. With three children to care for, book deadlines to meet, and a husband who was on the road for much of the time, the stay-at-home author often seemed overwhelmed. It was clear that she and Jeremy were not earning enough to afford the regular services of a housekeeper. And while Nancy did continue to employ Ulysses from Grate Patrol, his visits once every two weeks were nowhere near enough to return order to the family's jumbled living conditions.

As was typical of Jeremy, he did little to hide his disappointment with Nancy's housekeeping, and even criticized her in front of Don. He made it perfectly clear that he did not like that the house was so disorderly, and sometimes he even complained about her cooking as their dinner guest awkwardly looked on. If Nancy burned the chicken, Jeremy thought nothing of bluntly announcing: "This thing stinks!"

Even the children were not spared their father's wrath. Critical and stern, the former Marine captain routinely reprimanded Finny, Zeb, and Isabelle when they did not perform up to his standards. A bad grade was disciplined with a few blunt words—"I don't think you are smart enough!"—which were followed by a lecture on what steps Jeremy felt the child should take to improve.

Don found his friend's comments impolite, but not the least bit out of character. Through all of Jeremy's tirades, he noticed that Nancy never appeared afraid of her husband, and during their talks, she even admitted that she had always been attracted to his wild, unpredictable nature. Although his friend could be critical and discourteous at times, Don saw no signs that Jeremy was physically abusing his wife.

To Don and others, Jeremy fit the stereotypical profile of a macho man. He was domineering and gruff, and made it clear that he was afraid of nothing. Once he related a story to Don about how he had assaulted a pack of young hoodlums who had tried to rob him while he was out for a walk. The short, well-built Marine recounted how he did not let the mob of three intimidate him. When they tried to grab his wallet, he charged at them full force, getting in a few good punches before taking off on foot and outrunning them. Another time, Don learned that his obsession with physical fitness caused two of his dogs to die from heat stroke as they raced to keep up with him on a strenuous run through a local park. For weeks, Adam Lenkin and other neighbors on Reservoir Road wondered what had happened to the pair of muscular dogs that Jeremy kept tied to the tall white columns at the entrance to his home.

When his old law school roommate learned that his good friend had once been a cheerleader, dressed in a school uniform and shouting from the sidelines for his college football team, he did not believe it was true. Even Nancy found Jeremy's past as a cheerleader out of character and enjoyed teasing her husband, pulling out the yearbook and pointing to the pictures with uncontrollable laughter.

If Nancy was ever unhappy with Jeremy, she never admitted it to Don. Perhaps it was because Don was a friend of Jeremy's from law school, or perhaps there was another reason. An article published in *People* magazine after her death cited several telephone conversations that Nancy had with a friend shortly after she and Jeremy were married and moved to Florida. The story quoted an unidentified source as saying that during a late night telephone call, Nancy complained of abuse. And while it is unclear whether she meant abuse of a physical or mental nature, there were no police records to indicate that anything was amiss.

Don and others may not have known the extent of Nancy's unhappiness, because she always had a way of making even the most unpleasant situations seem as if they were perfectly acceptable. Over the course of her lifetime, she had become a master at recasting the negative circumstances of her life into challenges over which she was determined to triumph. She never spoke in the negative, and had almost a Pollyannaish way of rephrasing things that transformed even the most unpleasant event into one that sounded strangely positive—but made it difficult for anyone to know what she was honestly thinking or feeling. It was a quality that frustrated her friends, who suspected that

Nancy was bottling up her emotions in potentially harmful ways.

It was only after twenty years of marriage that Nancy finally admitted to herself that her relationship with Jeremy had grown increasingly difficult. Uncharacteristically, she confided to some of her trusted friends that the first five years of her marriage had been good, but that over the years that followed, things had slowly soured. Part of the problem, she rationalized, may have been the pressure that Jeremy felt to provide for his family. But to Don, Jeremy was still very much the same person he remembered sharing a house with outside Charlottesville. And Jeremy's other friends saw him as a man with raw talent at the top of his profession, but unwilling to dedicate his life to his work. An outdoorsman at heart, he thought nothing of putting important business on hold if an offer to ski, scuba dive, or hike came his way.

CHAPTER TEN

THE AKERS RESIDENCE SEEMED TO GET EVEN MESSIER with the arrival of Zeb and Isabelle. And Jeremy's at-home business added to the jumble. At first, he seemed to have his new work situation under control, but it slowly became apparent that he needed managerial help.

Who better than Nancy? But Nancy was saddled with the demands of her children and the deadlines of her budding writing career. Nevertheless, she complied when Jeremy asked her to type letters, address envelopes, and send faxes. The constant interruptions were maddening, and Nancy soon found herself wishing that her husband would be called away on a case.

Even more annoying was the way that Jeremy handled his billing. With no formal system in place, Nancy watched as he worked diligently on a project, racking up hundreds of billable hours. But when it came time to submit the itemized invoice, he procrastinated until their bank account dipped dangerously into the red. Unable to pay the rent, or any of the other household bills, Nancy begged Jeremy to write his bills out in longhand and promised to type them herself. But he ignored her pleas, and sometimes even left town to begin another assignment with thousands of dollars of uncollected monies out of Nancy's grasp. It infuriated her that he could be so irresponsible, knowing that he had three dependent children and a wife who didn't earn nearly enough to pay the household expenses.

But her aggravation did not end there. Nancy found it even more maddening that he refused to purchase health insurance for the family, citing his distrust for the companies that sell the policies. Instead, before he departed town for a job, Jeremy routinely handed Nancy an envelope stuffed with thousands of dollars in cash, and instructed her to use the money in case one of the children had to go to the hospital.

He continued to drive Nancy crazy when he was home between cases and constantly underfoot. As she struggled to get the kids off to school, stock the house with food, do the laundry, and get to the computer to work on her novels, her husband was spending his days lifting weights, jogging around the canal, and sunning himself on the rooftop.

Nancy found herself fighting to keep from falling into a depression. In addition to the family's financial pressures, she was distraught over her health and her displeasing physical appearance. With little time for exercise and food preparation, she snacked on junk food, all the while struggling to lose the weight she still retained from her pregnancies. Sometimes she resorted to ingesting a variety of diet and nutritional supplements and cutting down on her intake of food. But worrying about every calorie added even more stress to her already pressured life.

She was also growing restless with the Regencies that she was authoring, and found herself longing to write books that presented more of a challenge and promised greater financial rewards. Since *The Mayfair Season*, she had published *A Season Abroad*, which was released shortly after her first book in 1988. The story drew on her personal experiences as a college junior living abroad. *Philadelphia Folly*, her third book, was published as part of a new series of American Regency Romances from Warner. The idea behind the new series was to celebrate American high society and the true love

that blossomed on U.S. shores during the reign of England's
Prince Regent. She enjoyed researching the American Regency and excitedly kept friends like Mary Kilchenstein apprised as she familiarized herself with the intricacies of
paddleboat operations and the delicate patterns that adorned
the dishes and soup tureens of the era. She even regaled
Mary with humorous tales about the kind of family politics
that could have taken place at the dinner table at the time.

In January of 1990, Nancy celebrated the release of yet
another Regency, *The Lilac Garland*. At that time, she decided to terminate her relationship with her agent, Adele
Leone, and hired another firm to represent her work. In
1992, she added three more Regencies to her portfolio.
Fawcett Books released one of her new titles, *Devil's Wa-
ger*, while Avon Books published *Miss Wickham's Be-
trothal* and *Lady Sarah's Charade*. In spite of her success,
Nancy's advances were still small, amounting to little more
than $5,000 a book. Even the royalties she was receiving
were not enough to cover the cost of her young children's
private school tuition. Her parents had turned down her
request for financial assistance, so she was now faced with
the reality that her younger son was going to have to attend
public school.

Her ongoing struggle to keep up with the financial demands at home had her forever scheming up ways to earn
extra money. She tried everything from selling a line of
high-end makeup, to hosting shows at her home to market
the Christmas and holiday ornaments that she had collected
over the years. She sold stationery for the Junior League,
and in later years, she showcased the works of local crafts-
men and artists, presenting their wares with the promise of
a percentage of the evening's sales.

In fact, the very first time she spoke to romance writer
Ann Marie Winston on the telephone, Nancy tried to sell

her some makeup. The perky blonde had been advised to call Nancy, who had been past retreat chairwoman of the WRW, to get ideas for the 1991 weekend that she had been assigned to plan. As a writer of contemporary romances, it had taken Ann Marie two years to make her first sale. She had been ecstatic when she learned that a publisher had agreed to buy the fifth manuscript that she had written.

Although Nancy had all but stopped attending the monthly meetings, Ann Marie had heard that she had been instrumental in getting the weekend retreats off the ground during the organization's inaugural years. She was thrilled at the warm reception and good advice she received when she reached the author at home. She learned that Nancy was someone who could get things done. Over the years, she had earned a reputation as someone who was constantly coming up with innovative ways to promote herself and her books, and she graciously shared her strategies with members of the group. From what Ann Marie had heard, Nancy always showered promising words on young writers who called her for advice about pursuing their dreams.

"Believe in miracles!" she would tell them. The encouraging phrase had become Nancy's trademark.

In 1993, Nancy released *Lord Fortune's Prize*, her ninth Regency. She was also the year's recipient of the prestigious Bookrack Award. Yet somehow, the excitement of publication had begun to wane for Nancy. Forty-two years old, and overwhelmed by the responsibilities of raising two young children and a teenage boy, Nancy once again found herself fighting depression. She was also distraught over her weight, finding it impossible to believe that she was now buying Laura Ashley dresses in a size sixteen. For a woman standing barely five feet, four inches tall, the dress size was appalling. But worrying about everything she ate added even more stress to her already pressured life.

Nancy was also increasingly frustrated by the small advances that she was getting for her books, and was growing bored with writing the short, detail-filled paperbacks. While she had achieved formidable success in the genre, and took great pleasure in the extensive research that the Regencies required, she longed to write grander, more highly charged romances. Convinced that she was ready to take on a substantially bigger project, she attempted to write her first historical novel, a genre that was not limited to one particular time period—or less than two hundred pages—and in which she could write more explicit sex scenes than the traditional Regency allowed. Besides, historical novels promised unlimited financial rewards.

But her new endeavor proved eerily similar to the experience she had had with the contemporaries. Unable to write the kind of high-tension scenes that excite readers, Nancy once again turned to her talented and prolific friend, Kathy Seidel, for help.

Kathy had recently given birth to her second child, and she and Nancy had lost touch. It was good to hear her old friend's voice on the line, and after a few minutes of catching up, she listened as Nancy spelled out the reason for her call. Nancy said that what she had always liked about Kathy's writing were the scenes that evoked what she called "heart pang moments."

"You know, scenes in which you stir people's emotions," Nancy explained in her soft, even voice.

After some time on the line, Kathy urged her friend to consider writing about something that evoked a personal emotional response.

"Nancy, you've got to write about things that stir you in order to achieve those heart pang moments," Kathy explained. "What are you afraid of? What worries you?"

After a long silence, Nancy responded, "Oh, maybe I am just a superficial person."

The revelation surprised Kathy. She had always found Nancy warm and vibrant. She had seen the spirited brunette weave in and out of accents, share her generosity with friends, and exhibit great flamboyance and style in dress. She had always interpreted Nancy's intensity as a sign of someone capable of deep emotion. But suddenly Kathy realized that Nancy's dramatics and the passion she exhibited in front of invited guests, masked an inability to connect with people—or herself—on a deep emotional level.

Later that year, Nancy began work on a medieval trilogy for Avon. After two collaborations and seven Regencies, the larger composition would be her inaugural attempt at a full-length historical. Her first installment, *The Heart and the Heather*, set in Scotland, debuted in 1994.

The book's release was followed by the publication of *The Heart and the Rose* in 1995, and *The Heart and the Holly*, which was set in Ireland, completed the trio in the summer of 1996. Writing about the rich history of Ireland captivated Nancy, who had traveled to the country on a trip sponsored by *Romantic Times Magazine*, a fan publication, and whose personal library included more than three hundred books on Ireland.

"I started out as a political speechwriter, and while Capitol Hill may be light-years away from Irish warriors, poets, blanket bogs, *sidhe*, saints, green hills, and miracles, the distance between historical romance and Ireland isn't far," she was quoted as saying. "Irish history is rich with men and women whose lives were at once heroic, vivid, poignant, and worthy of inspiration for a romance writer.

"A lot of people ask me if I'd like to write 'real' historicals, and sure, that would be a challenge . . . but I do love historical romance and especially as a genre for Irish historicals because history can be depressing and dreary, dark, cold, dank, unliberated, and hopeless. But romance allows me to find the happy ending, to modify reality just enough to give it hope."

Nancy's larger works received kudos from reviewers, and were touted in advertisements by the Romance Writers of America. When she began work on *Wild Irish Skies*, her second historical romance set in Ireland, she had authored a total of ten books on her own.

Colleagues noticed that her more recent books had more depth and emotion, with more realistic characters and richer storylines. Yet, it was unclear to her fellow authors whether Nancy's writing had improved as a result of her determination to learn the trade, or if she had actually matured and was becoming emotionally astute herself. They also noticed that Nancy seemed to have triumphed over her weight problem. By the middle of 1996, the forty-five-year-old author had dropped more than thirty pounds. Her full face was now thin, almost gaunt from the strict regime of exercise and diet that she and her new friend Emily had been diligently following.

Nancy had met the tall, attractive brunette three summers before at the Mt. Vernon College swimming pool. The small, private women's college had recently merged with George Washington University. As an alumna of Mt. Vernon, Nancy was familiar with its location not far from her own home on the outskirts of bustling Georgetown. She was pleased to learn that the school had opened a spectacular aquatic facility to local residents and their families, and found it a convenient spot for her and her children to cool off during the steamy summer months of July and August.

On one particular afternoon, Nancy's daughter Isabelle befriended one of the young girls swimming in the shallow area of the pool. As the two children got to know each other, Nancy oversaw them, sitting fully clothed in a Laura Ashley dress, her polished toes dangling in the cool chlorinated water, her eyes hidden behind big, horn-rimmed sunglasses. Looking up from the manuscript she was editing, she noticed that the child's mother had joined the girls on the steps of the pool. Eventually, the two women struck up a casual conversation.

Flashing her thick, neatly typed manuscript at the forty-something mother with the short, stylish bob, Nancy grinned and went on to explain that she was an author, and that she was racing against a book deadline. She found it comforting to learn that Emily had three children of her own, worked in real estate sales, and lived nearby. Like Nancy, she had been raised in the Northeast, and had pursued a career in politics when she first moved to DC with her husband.

As the summer progressed, the two women and their children became good friends. Emily especially enjoyed her shopping expeditions with Nancy, and she found it amusing when Nancy repeatedly tried to sway her into loosening up her wardrobe by adding articles of clothing that were less conservative than the khakis and polo shirts she so loved.

When it was time to enroll their children in grade school, Emily chose Our Lady of Victory Elementary School, which was located on the corner of MacArthur Boulevard and Whitehaven Parkway, just up the street from Nancy's house on Reservoir Road. Zeb and Isabelle would later join Emily's children at the elementary school, which was run by Our Lady of Victory Catholic Church and attended by many of the children living in the neighborhood. The impressive house of worship featured an elaborately decorated arched wooden door, traditional New England–style steeple, and gracious stone-and-brick chapel. Perched atop a sloping hill, it boasted a breathtaking view of the reservoir. The adjacent parochial school had a more modern feel, with rows of rectangular-shaped windows adorned by colorful art projects and whimsical cutouts.

As Nancy's friendship with Emily strengthened, she confided that she was very unhappy about her size-sixteen figure. When the two women first met, Nancy weighed more than 150 pounds. Her new status as an author of historical romances required that she participate in book tours to promote her works, and it upset her greatly to appear before her fans as a frumpy old housewife with the thick calves and heavy thighs she had been battling to conceal for much of her adult life. Nancy was relieved when Emily confessed that she, too, had been struggling with her weight, and agreed to embark on an exercise and diet program with her. In spite of their full figures, both women were incredibly vain and neither allowed anyone to take their pictures.

Emily stood five feet, nine inches and weighed nearly 170 pounds when they began their weight loss program. At five feet, four inches, Nancy was aware that the extra weight she carried made her appear thicker-set and stouter than her friend.

Together, the two women began a strict diet that included careful monitoring of their caloric intake. They also joined the prominent Watergate Sport and Health Club, which was located nearby in the infamous Watergate Hotel—the scene of President Richard Nixon's ultimate downfall. The immaculate facility was located in the basement of the hotel and was equipped with a swimming pool, sauna, and gymnasium, and it offered its members a wide range of fitness classes including aerobics. Both Nancy and Emily became regulars at the health club, diligently weight-training in the state-of-the-art gym, and participating in as many aerobics classes as they could squeeze into their busy schedules.

Nancy's efforts paid off, with the author handing Emily,

who was now far along in a pregnancy, her collection of Laura Ashley size-sixteen dresses in 1996, announcing that she no longer needed them and joking that Emily could put them to use as maternity wear. Nancy had lost nearly thirty pounds, and had slimmed down to a perfect size six. She proudly showed off her hourglass figure with a new wardrobe of dresses that she wore cinched at the waist. The woman who had spent the last ten years in loose-fitting dresses was buying pretty white petticoat skirts and colorful crinkle shirts to wear with lace-up Victorian-style high-heeled boots. Her newfound confidence even prompted her to let down her thick locks of wavy dark hair and wear them in wild ringlets that hung down to the middle of her back.

Her fellow authors were stunned when Nancy appeared at an emergency meeting of the Washington Romance Writers in 1996 to discuss a lawsuit that had been filed against the group and its current president, Mary Kilchenstein, by one of its board members. In a show of support for her former collaborator, Nancy marched straight to the front of the room. As she addressed the crowd in her gentle, bird-like voice, members noticed that she appeared thin to the point of illness. Although slender, her face was sallow and drawn. But in spite of her fragile appearance, she was energetic in her delivery, urging members to rally behind the organization and against the person who was threatening it. An enthusiastic round of applause and warm embraces followed her speech. Many of the women had not seen Nancy in years. After she began publishing with Avon, she had become less active in the group. In fact, the last Harpers Ferry retreat that she had attended was the one organized by Ann Marie Winston in 1991. That weekend, she had led a Regency genre workshop for the membership, which had more than doubled since the group was founded in the mid-80s. And while for the most part Nancy was well liked, she could also be a snob, especially toward people whose backgrounds, in her mind, were decidedly déclassé.

She did not understand people from "small-town America" and her naïveté—or perhaps a streak of mean-spiritedness—may have been what prompted her to refer to them as "hillbillies" behind their backs. The distrust between Nancy and certain members of the group seemed to go both ways. More than a few authors were turned off by what they perceived to be her snooty, elitist attitude, and offended by her constant name-dropping. To many, Nancy's ongoing friendship with society maven Patricia Duff—by then the wife of Revlon cosmetics billionaire Ronald Perelman—was of little interest to the women. But to others, word that Nancy was a close friend of Suzanne Martin Kent Cooke—wife of mogul John Kent Cooke— and that she and her children had attended her daughter Jacqueline's first birthday party at the couple's elegant, 4,400-square-foot townhouse made quite an impression.

Nancy's naïve presumption that everybody she associated with shared her political sentiments also surprised people. On more than one occasion, she had offended friends when she launched into a heated political discussion or invited them to a Republican fundraiser, never imagining— or caring—that they might hold contrary views. Nancy's husband was even stauncher in his politics. When Bill Clinton was elected to the White House in 1992, Jeremy locked himself in the bedroom, drew the curtains, and turned off all of the lights in silent protest. His loathing of the President's liberal politics, and the fact that he had dodged the draft and did not serve his country in Vietnam, incited Jeremy to heckle him during a speech Clinton gave at the National Mall. With his young son perched on his shoulders, he shouted at the President, confident that Zeb's presence would keep the Secret Servicemen at bay. Years later, Jeremy would return to the National Mall to take his own life.

CHAPTER ELEVEN

WHEN NANCY ARRIVED AT A BLACK-TIE GALA THAT WAS being hosted by one of Jeremy's friends in the fall of 1997, everybody in the room turned to stare. The couple was among the one hundred guests Bill Ranger invited to Morton's restaurant to celebrate his Commissioning as an officer in the U.S. Naval Reserves, an event he had waited for for twenty years. Dressed elegantly in a low-cut emerald-green gown bedecked with sequins that drew attention to her hourglass figure and sexy cleavage, Nancy was the hit of the affair.

The summer before, she had taken a friend's advice and checked into the hospital for plastic surgery that included a lift of her breasts and buttocks, and correction of her sagging eyelids. The results had turned an attractive middle-aged mother into a stunning beauty who exuded more self-confidence than she had ever felt before.

Thirty years after her first debutante ball, Nancy was coming out again, this time as a forty-six-year-old knockout with a figure that rivaled those of women half her age. She wore her lengthy black hair in elegant ringlets, and expensive French cosmetics decorated her now-youthful face. When she glided across the roomful of partygoers, even Bill Ranger did not recognize her. It was not until he saw her grab onto Jeremy's arm that he realized who she was. Even Jeremy, who was dapper in a stylish black tuxedo pinned with seven of the medals he had earned as a Marine, could not take his eyes off his wife.

But Nancy had all but lost interest in her husband of twenty years. She had grown weary of remaining faithful to a man whom she was certain had had more than one extra-marital affair. Jeremy's routine of traveling for weeks, sometimes months at a time, his willingness to attend social events and parties without her, and his criticism about her weight and the way she looked, had creaked in her a gnawing fear that he was seeing other women—a suspicion that she repeatedly shared with close friends. And while she could never confirm her suspicions of infidelity—she was fed up with trying to keep the household running and the bills paid while Jeremy was off jogging around the reservoir or playing a game of pick-up basketball at a neighborhood park. And she was tired of having to leave the answering machine on all the time to screen their calls for bill collectors and creditors.

For nearly two decades, she had endured endless criticisms about the way she kept the house, the weight she had put on as a result of her pregnancies, and the food that she served for dinner. It seemed that for as long as she could remember, everything she did was calculated not to upset her husband. She had held her tongue when he spent the rent money on extravagant toys for himself, or when he jaunted off to the Bahamas on a scuba trip when he should have been in his law office tending to his cases. And she'd grown tired of Jeremy's quirkiness: his refusal to buy health insurance, his endless procrastination for billing clients, and his bizarre need to collect and save everything from handfuls of leaflets he grabbed on his way out of the bank to knick-knacks rescued from the neighbors' trash. He could not part with anything—egg cartons, old phone books, even food—for fear he might need them someday. Even his refusal to redeem his frequent flier miles drove her crazy. And that he preferred to keep his money under his mattress rather than entrust it to a bank or financial institution. Nancy wanted to move to a bigger, more comfortable house with five bedrooms and a family room, but the deal never materialized because Jeremy refused to disclose to the landlord any information about his income or finances. On the near side of fifty, she no longer wanted to be living in a house that was in disrepair, with chipping paint, and old, unreliable appliances.

To make matters worse, Nancy had no quiet time to write. Jeremy's home office meant that he was always underfoot, interrupting her time and again to ask for help while she was trying to crank out yet one more book at her computer.

Her children also had needs. Zeb and Isabelle were like every other boy and girl their age, and were constantly asking their mom and dad for one thing or another. Yet, somehow, Jeremy never seemed to have time for anything more than a carefree trip to the park, which forced Nancy to limit her writing time to the hours after the children had gone to sleep.

Nancy's life had reached a turning point. Though her marriage was in tatters, her career was on an upward trajectory. The books that she wrote in the wee hours of the morning were generating critical acclaim from reviewers. *The Washington Post Book World* named *Wild Irish Skies* one the top five romances of 1997. She skillfully promoted her novels by going on book tours, organizing mass mailings using post cards of her book covers, and sending the owners of small specialty stores autographed posters depicting her latest book. She also networked through "Avon Ladies," an online chat group of authors who shared the same publisher. For the first time in her life, she was feeling physically gorgeous and intellectually fulfilled, attracting attention in ways she never had before.

The dynamics of Nancy's life at home with Jeremy were also changing. For years, she and Finny had enjoyed a special bond. As an only child for the first eleven years of his life, he was the closest to her of the three children. Nancy had always been able to count on Finny's help around the house when Jeremy was out of town on business. Even more important, he served as an emotional buffer between his parents. But in high school, Finny left home to attend Episcopal High School, a boarding school across the Potomac in Alexandria, Virginia. He had been enrolled at the Landon School; a pricey all-boys' school in Bethesda, Maryland, but his academic performance there disappointed his father, who had hoped that his son would gain entrance to a top-tier college and the U.S. Naval Academy. But an Ivy League education was not what Finny had in mind. He confided to his mother that when he completed his high school studies, he didn't want to go right off to college.

Rather than getting upset with her son, Nancy went to work crafting what could best be described as a makeshift sabbatical for Finny. After countless phone calls, she arranged for her son to spend one year out west doing wildlife conservation work, something he had always dreamed about doing. His father even surprised Finny with a scuba diving trip to the Bahamas as a high school graduation gift.

With Finny away at boarding school, and then out west on his furlough, he was unavailable to pick up the slack for his father and the problems between Nancy and Jeremy grew more pronounced. Nancy had lost an important source of emotional strength with Finny's departure and it didn't help that he preferred spending weekends on the campus with his friends. When he returned home for winter break, he noticed that his mother was spending an enormous amount of time on the Internet and wracking up huge bills from America Online.

Finny was keenly aware that in addition to his private school tuition and the tuition of his brother and sister at parochial school, his parents were struggling to pay the household bills and make payments on the family cars. He watched his mother struggling to help make ends meet, staying up late and getting up early in the morning to meet her deadlines, and he noticed her increased irritability and hair-trigger temper. He couldn't figure out if her bad mood was the result of the family's financial problems, or, the thought crossed his mind, that she might be going through a "change of life."

But one thing was certain: his father's quirky behavior was bothering his mother more than it had in the past. After living for years with a man who was so set in his ways, and so inflexible in his views, it was clear that his mother was reaching her breaking point. Finny knew she was tired of the way his father intimidated and offended people with his brusque and confrontational behavior and that she had run out of patience with other shortcomings.

Nancy's relationship with her own mother and brothers had fallen victim to her marriage to Jeremy, but unlike Finny, her younger children had no knowledge of the family's history. Friends who knew Nancy in her younger years remembered that her self-esteem was low when she married her husband, and her feelings of self-worth had not improved during the course of their twenty-year union. Searching for love and acceptance, Nancy had even been spotted in 1998 at a fundraiser in Manhattan, where she gave the impression that she was desperately trying to capture all the male attention she could.

But Nancy found a new social outlet in online chat rooms and emails. She no longer had the time to present workshops to aspiring authors, but she had a satisfying substitute on the Web. Ever the innovator, she had created and was the administrator of her own Website at a time when others were still learning how to surf the World Wide Web and Internet. Through her own site, and through the Avon Ladies, she traded expertise with others in her field and offered career guidance to fledgling authors who paid her with free advice on Website design. She was determined to promote herself and her latest books online and found herself participating as a guest author in literary chat rooms and running contests that offered autographed first-edition copies of her novels as prizes. Her efforts were paying dividends. Old fans were finding her online and others were discovering her.

"All my fiction is inspired by real life," Nancy acknowledged about herself on her Website. Adding: "Nancy will never cease to marvel at the wonder of working at home to spin tales of faraway places, forgotten times, heroic men and courageous, self-aware heroines."

James Lemke, a truck driver from Chicago, Illinois, found Nancy in 1997 through an online search. Friends and relatives recount two different stories about how Nancy and Jim first met. Some say the two first started communicating in a poetry chat room. But author Mary Kilchenstein says that Nancy told her that Jim had been trying to find Mary Kirk, the author of *A Phoenix Rising*, a contemporary romance novel about a long-haul trucker. A friend had given him the book to read, and he had identified with the story's hero. He decided he wanted to find more about the book's author, so he punched in her name and found a link to Nancy's Website. Because Nancy had collaborated with Mary Kilchenstein on two books that were published under the name Mary Alice Kirk, her Website popped up in Lemke's search. Flattered by his interest in the novel,

Nancy struck a conversation with the young man who dubbed himself the "poet king."

Not until later did she reveal that she was not the author of the book that he so admired, but rather her friend Mary Kilchenstein, who had published subsequent novels under the pseudonym Mary Kirk. The revelation did not stop the correspondence between Nancy and her new Internet friend. The two began emailing each other on a regular basis. At first, their conversation centered on Nancy's career as a writer, and Jim's aspirations as a poet. As the weeks passed, however, she began reading and critiquing his poems and short stories. Twenty-six years old and recently divorced, Jim was eager to pursue a writing career and Nancy was happy to oblige. Helping aspiring writers was something she had done for years.

Nancy's coaching proved fruitful and Jim's poetry showed signs of improvement. The stream of emails also provided the truck driver with a glimpse into Nancy's personal life, and her relationship with her husband. Nancy portrayed Jeremy as "controlling," and told her online friend that she was frightened of him.

The paunchy young truck driver had recently moved back home to Chicago to live with his mother, also named Nancy. After his divorce from Jennifer Dietrich, who was three years his senior, he left their condominium on West Touhy Avenue in Niles, Illinois, and, despairing over his failed marriage, had sought comfort and companionship online. During the months that he stayed with his mom in her apartment on North Monitor Avenue, he talked often about his budding electronic relationship with the famous romance author and described how she had helped to improve his children's poetry and short stories.

In March 1998, Jim decided to quit his job and move to the Capital City to be closer to his mentor—and to help her in her difficult relationship with her husband.

Nancy was excited about her friend's arrival, and invited him to stay with the family in their home on Reservoir Road. Jeremy was out of town on an assignment the week that Jim pulled up in front of the stately two-story brick colonial. The chemical company, Monsanto, had hired him, and his new assignment had him traveling back and forth to Louisiana. Zeb and Isabelle liked their mother's new visitor. They found him easy-going, fun, and interested in their hobbies and activities.

When Jeremy returned, Nancy passed her new house-guest off as the son of a romance writer friend, and said that he would be staying with them for a few weeks until he found a place to live. At first, Jeremy accepted Jim into his home, even inviting him to jog on his daily runs. But as the days passed, he grew increasingly suspicious of his houseguest, and at one point even asked him if he was involved with Nancy. "Are you f—king my wife?" he demanded to know.

"No, frankly, she's too old for me," the "poet king" responded.

The response seemed to appease Jeremy, and Jim continued to stay with the family while he looked for work and an apartment. In subsequent conversations with Nancy's husband, Jim detailed his stormy relationship with his ex-wife and confided that he intended to exert complete control over the next woman who came into his life.

But while the Akerses' younger children were enthusiastic about having Jim around the house, the connection between Jeremy and Nancy grew increasingly strained. Nancy told Jim that she was growing more and more frightened of her husband. Even Jim's mother, whom he regularly called, believed from his reports that something in the house was amiss. He always telephoned her before he went

jogging with Jeremy to make sure that she was aware of
his whereabouts in case she heard he had suddenly gone
"missing."

Soon after his arrival, Jim secured a job as a truck driver
for Coca-Cola, and with Nancy's help, found a small one-
bedroom apartment in the basement of a nondescript five-
story building just down the street, within walking distance
of the Akers house. Its residents were mostly blue-collar
folk, but the building had more than its share of problems.
Over the years, the police had been called to the location
to investigate accusations of drug possession and dealing
by its renters. Jim continued to spend time with Nancy,
Jeremy, and the kids after he moved out. He even continued
jogging with Jeremy.

But the relationship between Nancy and Jeremy seemed
to worsen by the day. Jim's mother would later reveal that
Nancy complained to her online about being physically
abused by her husband. The three of them—Jim, Nancy,
and Jim's mother—often chatted online simultaneously using AOL's "Instant Message" service. One evening, Nancy
Lemke was online with her son when Nancy Akers joined
the two of them to chat. It had been a few days since Mrs.
Lemke had last talked to Nancy, who had been ill with the
flu. Jim's mother immediately asked Nancy how she was
feeling and was glad to learn that she was on the mend.
But after a short while, Nancy suddenly announced that she
had to go because Jeremy was worrying about her and
wanted her to get back into bed to rest. "That's funny that
he's worried about now," Nancy typed. "He is probably
trying to make up for throwing me up against the bathroom
door last week."

In April, Jim accompanied Nancy to the Washington Romance Writers Retreat in Harpers Ferry. Nancy was scheduled to present a workshop entitled "Character vs. Action—

The Salable Synopsis." The year before, she had given a talk on "How Unpublished Authors Sabotage Their Manuscripts," and had participated in a panel discussion along with her friend Kathy Seidel. But unlike the previous year, Nancy did not come to West Virginia for the entire weekend. Instead, she showed up at the Hilltop House a few hours before she was scheduled to speak on Sunday with her young friend Jim in tow. Many of the writers found it strange that Nancy introduced the young man with the thin mustache simply as her "protector."

"Oh, he's my bodyguard," Nancy told author Mary Kilchenstein after she spotted Jim standing in a doorway, watching Nancy make a presentation. Mary had no idea what to make of Nancy's comment, or why in the world she would ever need a bodyguard.

As he stood in the doorway admiring Nancy from a distance, Jim turned to Mary and asked: "Isn't she just the most wonderful, brilliant person you've ever seen?" From his comment, it was clear to Mary that the man was something more than simply a bodyguard to Nancy.

But Mary never had a chance to ask her close friend what was going on because Nancy and Jim left right after the lecture ended. Mary could only wonder about her friend's bizarre statement, and the comment the young man in the faded blue jeans and worn cowboy boots had made.

Several of the writers who were in attendance that weekend recall that Nancy and Jim toured the grounds of the historic hotel together before taking off for Washington. Others remember Nancy mentioning that she and her friend had been staying at a hotel down the road.

As the weeks passed, Jeremy grew even more suspicious. Once again, he confronted Jim about his relationship with Nancy. This time the twenty-six-year-old told him that Nancy had never made a pass at him, but that, if she ever did, he would find it hard to turn her down. The comment infuriated Jeremy, who had been wary of the young man for some time. When he subsequently confronted his wife, Nancy continued to maintain that her relationship with Jim was platonic. It was a story that she would tell even her closest confidantes.

But Jeremy remained suspicious—and continued to question his wife and several of her close friends about her ongoing friendship with the out-of-towner. By June, he had all but lost interest in his legal practice. Convinced that there was more to his wife's friendship than she was letting on, Jeremy began to watch Nancy closely, taking on the role of investigator as he followed them around town recording their movements in an attempt to prove his suspicion of adultery.

In spite of her denials, even Nancy's friends began to suspect that the two were having an affair, a fact that was confirmed for her friend Emily one night when Isabelle called shortly before 9 p.m. to ask if her mother was still there doing the family's laundry. The young girl's phone call caught her completely off guard. While Nancy had been coming over to use Emily's machine on a regular basis, because her own dryer had been breaking down, that was not the case the night that Isabelle called. In fact, Emily did not know where the girl's mother was, and was left wondering how her friend could leave her two young children home alone at that hour.

The situation worsened when Jeremy returned home from a business trip and discovered what a friend said was evidence that his wife and Jim had been making love in the family residence. Infuriated, he reportedly confronted Nancy with his suspicions. She insisted that nothing was going on, but friends say he was unconvinced and lashed out at her, badly bruising her eye. Jeremy later confided that he had a hard time coming to grips with the fact that he had lost his temper, and struck his wife. In an emotional encounter, he subsequently described the battle to friends, sought forgiveness, and struggled to come up with some way to apologize for what he had done. He insisted that it was the only time he had ever raised a hand to his wife. His friends believed he was sincere, but said that, as devout Catholics, they could not condone his violent behavior. Later, they would learn that Jeremy did have a tendency to be verbally abusive, and in the last several years, might have actually shoved his wife during disagreements and arguments at the family home. Her face battered and swollen from the blow she had sustained, Nancy began to tell her friends that Jeremy had been physically abusive and cruel to her for much of their marriage.

Even before the incident, friends say that Nancy and Jeremy slept in separate bedrooms. Friends reported that at Nancy's suggestion, the couple bought a new dining room table to keep in their bedroom to be used as Jeremy's new workspace. Her feeling was that it was preferable for him to dump his papers there, out of sight. Once it was installed, however, she claimed that the clutter was too much for her and that it prompted her to start sleeping on the couch in the spare room upstairs. She also moved her own desk out of her first-floor office—to Jim's house—claiming that she couldn't get any writing done at home.

In August, Jim's mother drove from Chicago to Washington to spend a week visiting with her son. Jeremy was out of town, and Nancy was home with Isabelle. Zeb had gone down to Alabama to stay with his grandparents, and Isabelle had an airplane reservation to join him there later that week. Jim excitedly introduced his mother to the author he had moved to the District to be near. Already, the two women had one thing in common—their age! They were both born in 1951.

Nancy Lemke found the romance writer prettier and even more intelligent than her son had described, and the heavy-set woman grew to like her even better after her whirlwind tour of the Capital. With Nancy Akers playing tour guide, they visited the White House, the Capitol building, and various museums, taking special care to avoid the city's seedier neighborhoods. The expedition left Nancy Lemke breathless, and gushing about how smart her son's friend was. She was even treated to a visit to the author's comfortable residence, which she found to be well-appointed and full of exquisite antiques.

While Nancy Lemke was in town, Nancy Akers, strangely, opted to take Isabelle to sleep in Jim's modest one-bedroom apartment, rather than having everyone stay in her spacious home. But friends of the author deny that Nancy ever permitted Isabelle to spend the night in Jim's apartment. During the visit, Mrs. Lemke took an intense liking to Isabelle, and laughed as Jim and Nancy joked about the little girl's loquaciousness.

Later that week, Nancy put Isabelle on a flight to Alabama, and waved Jim's mother a farewell. Days later, she phoned Jeremy, who had joined the children in Sheffield, to say that she would be moving out. Stunned, Jeremy offered to leave the kids in Alabama with his parents, enroll them in school there, and fly back to Washington to try to work things out with his wife. But Nancy rebuffed his offer. She decided instead to take the advice of a close friend and insist that Jeremy and the children return to the District. She was convinced that her friend was right in saying that Zeb and Isabelle would be better off with their parents, even though Nancy seemed poised to ask for a divorce. She feared that if she allowed the children to remain in Alabama with Jeremy's family, she could lose them for good.

Bewildered, Jeremy telephoned one of Nancy's friends and pleaded with her to give him some insight into what was going on. He was uncertain of exactly what had gone wrong, and wondered if his wife's decision to leave was fueled by a hormonal imbalance triggered by menopause. He admitted to the woman that he had not always been faithful, and that he had not always been there for his wife, but vowed to do whatever he could to make the relationship work.

When the children returned to Washington, and learned that their mother had moved in with Jim, they were confused. At first, Zeb turned on his father and blamed him for his mother's departure. The ten-year-old boy had grown extremely fond of Jim since his arrival in the District five months before. He felt that he found a friend in the young truck driver and it pleased him to see his mother so happy whenever Jim was around. For young Isabelle, the situation was more complicated. Like her brother, she liked and admired Jim. But she was upset when she saw how devastated her father was over the departure of her mother and did what she could to comfort him.

Finny, too, had a difficult time understanding what had happened. Growing up, he had always believed that his parents had been happy. When he finally realized that his mother was disenchanted with her marriage, he thought it was just another problem that his parents would work out. He was aware of his mother's frustration over his father's chronic procrastination, and the idiosyncrasies that set him apart from the rest of the world, but he thought of his father's quirkiness as a quality that made him unique.

But his hope that his parents would resurrect their marriage was dashed when Nancy moved out of the house. Nevertheless, Finny was encouraged when his father continued to persuade Nancy to stay in close contact with him and the younger children, inviting her to come over to the house on a daily basis to help send them off to school in the morning and to assist them with their homework at night. Jeremy's only condition was that Nancy keep the children away from Jim. He asked that she not bring her lover into the family home, and forbade her to take Zeb and Isabelle to Jim's apartment.

Jeremy was not alone in his expectations of Nancy. Her best friend Emily also let her know that her lover was not welcome in her house because of the unwholesome example it would present to her children.

But Jeremy's pleadings fell on deaf ears. At one point Nancy tried to take Zeb and Isabelle to Jim's apartment, but made it only as far as the building's basement hallway before Isabelle went into a state of shock and fell screaming to the floor. Annoyed, Nancy tossed the kids back in the car and took them home. On the way, she told them that they had to come to grips with her decision and accept Jim.

All the while, Jeremy seemed determined to change. The man whom many regarded as selfish and self-centered seemed genuinely determined to put his own needs aside in the interest of caring for his children—and possibly saving his marriage. Even his closest friends were surprised when he made his children's welfare his top priority. He repeatedly asked his wife to come to the house and meet with him to talk through some of their problems for the sake of the children. But time after time, she wound up picking a fight with him and storming out in a huff, often in front of Zeb and Isabelle.

For the first time in his life, Jeremy was confronted with a situation that was totally beyond his control, and that he could not seem to fix, no matter how hard he tried. Even his apologies and promises to change did not sway Nancy.

Finny and his siblings were convinced that Jim was at the root of their mother's odd behavior. The children suspected that Jim was controlling her actions and trying to drive a wedge between their mother and them. It was difficult for Finny to watch as his father telephoned his mother and pleaded with her to come over and talk it out. He could see how utterly destroyed he was at the prospect of losing his family. He was also surprised at how his father had changed after Nancy moved out. The gruff Marine corps mentality was gone, replaced by a new, gentler man who was open—indeed, desperate—to reconcile with his wife. To make matters worse, Finny could not understand his mother's flat-out refusal to listen to his dad's pleas and find it in her heart to give the man who had been her husband for the last twenty years one more chance.

All at once, both his parents seemed like strangers to him. His father was uncharacteristically mournful and compliant, while his mother's refusal to listen to reason was also out of character. It troubled the young man that his mother could be so black and white, seeing things from her perspective only and not in the gray tones of compromise. After all, Finny thought, she and his father had raised three children together, and they weren't even grown yet! He wondered how any mother could overlook that important fact.

Yet, while Finny was heartsick over what was going on at home, he did notice that something good had come from his mother's decision to leave. The young man observed that Nancy seemed happier and more relaxed away from his dad. He was also surprised to learn that she had begun communicating with his grandmother, Susan Richards, after years of near silence between the two women.

Roderick and Susan Richards barely even knew their two youngest grandchildren. But the news that Nancy had finally broken away from her husband caused her parents to rejoice. They listened with keen interest as she explained that her new friend, Jim, had been instrumental in helping her to find the courage to free herself from Jeremy. From the way their daughter spoke of her new friend, they were convinced that Jim was a knight in shining armor who had rescued their little princess from her mean and evil husband. They were so jubilant, in fact, that they even offered to help pay Zeb and Isabelle's parochial school tuition.

Meanwhile, Jeremy was struggling to come to terms with the new man in Nancy's life. He had thought for certain that his wife would come to her senses, once she realized how inadequate her young lover was in comparison to both him and the other substantial men she knew. Not only was Jim Lemke less than half his age, he was the exact opposite of everything that Jeremy Akers stood for. Jeremy was appalled at how out of shape Jim was, that he wore one earring, that he was uneducated, and earned a living at the wheel of a heavy truck. He wondered how his wife could possibly fall for such a person. But his real concern was the message that her relationship with this man was sending to his children.

He did not want his children in contact with this man, and vowed to do whatever he could to protect them from Jim. To Jeremy, under no circumstances would his children live under the same roof as Jim. He repeatedly offered to give Nancy custody of Zeb and Isabelle—*if* she would move out of Jim's apartment and into a place of her own, that he would pay for. He even offered to pay her other household expenses. But Nancy, who so often had been forced to take on extra work to pay the family's bills, refused.

On Wednesday, October 7, 1998, Nancy's last novel, *So*

Wild a Kiss, was shipped to bookstores across the country. In it, she thanked the "poet king"—Jim Lemke.

> *To all those women down through Irish history who have aided the Queen on her way to Freedom, especially to the memory of those whose lives inspired this work: Eleanor, Countess of Desmond; Eibhlin Dhubh ní Chonaill; Lady Wilde, Maud Gonne; Mairead Farrell; and Constance Markievicz.*

> *To the centuries of poets, who, in daring to open their hearts and souls, have preserved moments in time too precious to be forgotten, and especially, to the poet king.*

Acknowledging Jim in her novel was quite a statement for Nancy, who had not dedicated any of her books to her husband (although a character in one of her earlier novels had been an Earl named Jeremy).

The same week that *So Wild a Kiss* was hitting the bookshelves, Nancy sent an electronic email to her old friend Mary Kilchenstein. In it, she provided her former collaborator with some insight into her life.

Subj: Re:??
Date: 10/11/98 11:35:19 AM Eastern Daylight Time
From: Nancy Akers
To: Marykilch

Hi Mary,
Now as to my move . . . the long story goes over a 15 year period; the shorter version over the past 24 months, but in a nutshell, I had been lying and hiding the truth of my marriage for many years, and as the

situation deteriorated and yes, the abuse became worse, I could no longer pretend or cope and finally, got brave enough to say I wanted out despite the death threats . . . yes, it reads worse than a bad novel. My best friend Emily and my writer friend Jim both kind of pushed me along . . . and Jim for awhile was literally my physical protection . . . sort of like a bodyguard as at Harpers Ferry. Jeremy refused to leave the house—although he said in June that maybe sometime after the first of the year he might move . . . The situation was intolerable and really bad on writing with office in house . . . had been impossible for about two years which is one reason it took me so long to finish KISS . . . Anyway, on August 1 I moved my office to Jim's apartment with the understanding that I would only live in the house so long as the children were also in the house. That situation deterioarated [sic] and I don't sleep there anymore . . . I go at 5 AM to get Zeb and Isabelle ready for school and do their lunches; then again at night for homework and bedtime etc etc but that may soon end too since Jeremy continues to be abusive to me, and I have a lawyer who—I think is going to tell me that for reasons that I would go into but I am already rambling. I don't mind talking about this or people knowing, it is just that telling someone about all of this is kind of like dropping an A-bomb and then running for cover. Anyway, I can be reached during the day at 202-XXX-XXXX; I am doing much better away from Jeremy, and Zeb and Isabelle are safe with him in terms of physical safety, but my lawyer is going to get them away from him because that is what I want. Anyway, long story into short email comes out kind of stranger than it should . . . Byeeee for now, Nancy

"Byeeee for now" was the way that Nancy signed all of her online correspondence. And while the author's note to Mary—and to other writers at Avon—clearly implied that Nancy had been exposed to years of abuse at the hands of her husband, Finny and others insist that the allegations are just not true. Nancy's oldest son said that not once did he ever see his father raise a hand to his mother.

One month after Nancy's letter to Mary, on November 15, 1998, the police were called to the Akers residence. Patrol officers from the Metropolitan Police Department's Second District squared their shoulders and listened as the man and woman who answered the front door described an argument that had sent Nancy to the phone to dial 911. Uniformed in the city's official navy slacks and light-blue collared shirts, the two officers stood on the front stoop of the gracious red-brick residence and jotted down notes.

At one point Nancy pleaded with the officers to help her take the children from the house. But she was advised that that was not the proper thing to do and that she should go through the courts.

An Incident Report was filed with the department in which the officers detailed their findings. In their report, they noted that the couple had been married and was currently separated. They had become engaged in a verbal dispute after Jeremy sought to taunt Nancy by blocking passage at the doorway that Nancy was attempting to exit. Neither party made a case for physical assault, nor did the officers observe any signs of physical abuse. According to department policy, the officers would have been required to make an arrest if there was any indication that there had been a physical assault.

It would not be the last time that officers would be summoned to the scene. On June 5, 1999, they would again be called to 4632 Reservoir Road, only this time the circumstances would be far more grisly.

CHAPTER TWELVE

AS THE FIGHTING BETWEEN NANCY AND JEREMY CONTINued, their children wondered why their mother was so unwilling to entertain their father's continuous pleas for reconciliation. A pattern seemed to be emerging in which Jeremy would attempt to engage his wife in a friendly discussion, when suddenly she would fly off the handle and begin shouting at him. Within minutes, their conversation would blow up into a raging fight.

When Zeb saw that his father was trying so hard, and that his mother was refusing to give him a chance, he demanded to know why she was being so cruel.

"Why aren't you even trying?" the boy asked to no avail. Frustrated, he began withdrawing from his mother and increasingly sided with his dad.

Zeb grew even angrier when he called Jim's apartment and asked to speak to his mother, only to be told that he first had to say "please." When he hesitated, the trucker hung up the phone, leaving the ten-year-old with just the sound of the dial tone.

Jim felt that the children had turned on him after their mother moved in with him. When they called the apartment and he answered, they would simply say, "Put my mother on the line," and then start yelling at him for taking her away. The quarrel with the kids got so bad that he installed a second phone line for himself.

On December 25, 1998, Jim's mother telephoned the

Akers house. She had heard that Nancy was celebrating the holiday with her children and wanted to wish her a Merry Christmas. When Jeremy answered the telephone, Mrs. Lemke asked to speak with Nancy.

"Who's this?" he demanded.

"Nancy," Mrs. Lemke replied.

"Yeah, right," Jeremy responded sarcastically and hung up the phone.

Soon after New Year's Day, Nancy went to see one of the city's top divorce attorneys. But when she learned the man's fee, she asked if he could refer her to a less expensive lawyer. She was given the name of Alan Soschin. The stocky, well-educated man from New Jersey had practiced as a criminal attorney in the District for much of his twenty-six-year career, but had made a gradual switch to family law.

When Nancy went to see him, he was still in his office near the DC court complex. The walls of his downtown suite were decorated with artists' sketches of courtroom scenes, and a framed bachelor's degree he had received from Lehigh University in 1969. As Nancy detailed her situation, the attorney took notes. He listened as the clearly angry author matter-of-factly explained that she had been the one to move out of the family house, and gave her new address as 4840 MacArthur Boulevard. Nancy also described the stormy relationship she had shared with Jeremy Akers, and his history of violence during their twenty-year union.

In spite of her allegations of abuse, Mr. Soschin noted that his client did not seem afraid of her husband, believing that she thought she had escaped the danger when she moved out of the house on Reservoir Road. Yet, she did not seem concerned—or afraid—about going back each morning to ready the children for school, and returning in the afternoons to help Zeb and Isabelle with their homework.

As their initial consultation continued, Nancy expressed her desire for sole or joint custody of her two minor children, and her need for spousal support. While her books were being well received by the romance-fiction fans, her earnings remained small. *So Wild a Kiss* fetched an advance that barely exceeded $10,000. To make up for the small stipend, she had resorted to selling evening bags and other handmade crafts.

The divorce lawyer advised Nancy that the District of Columbia had equitable distribution laws, and that in cases where there are children involved, most judges leaned toward joint custody—unless there is a history of domestic violence.

Mr. Soschin realized the Akerses' divorce would not be an easy one to settle. Nancy and her husband were barely talking to each other and the couple did not have enough money to keep two households running at the same time.

Jeremy, too, sought legal counsel. He met with several of Washington's top lawyers, but quickly learned that he could not afford their services. In an effort to save money, he decided to try his case *pro se*, to represent himself. Jeremy's family appealed to him to reconsider, and to let them pay for the attorney. But he repeatedly rejected their pleas.

Meanwhile, Nancy began sending out email messages to fellow authors in New Hampshire, North Carolina, and Colorado describing the "abuse" she had suffered at the hands of her husband.

"I could not take it any longer, and told my husband I wanted a divorce," she wrote to one author. "He broke my nose . . . and I suffered black eyes." Friends said they believe that Nancy was referring to the day that Jeremy struck her after learning of her affair with Jim Lemke.

On February 26, 1999, Jeremy Ray Akers was served by special process with *A Complaint for Legal Separation from Bed and Board, Custody, Child Support and Spousal Support.*

Nancy's contention, according to the legal papers, was that the deterioration of the marriage was detrimental to the health and well-being of the children, as well as to herself. "The Defendant's conduct towards her constitutes cruelty and the Plaintiff is unable and unwilling to continue the marital relationship between the parties and sacrifice her health, safety, and self-respect," the papers read. "Defendant's cruel conduct directed at the Plaintiff includes, but is not limited to: unpredictable and random actions including, but not limited to alienation of the children, extreme verbal abuse, ongoing taunting and insults, death threats, physical and emotional intimidation and assault."

As for financial arrangements, Nancy's complaint read, "The Defendant is an attorney who is currently self-employed as an environmental consultant and investigator. His income is far superior to that of the Plaintiff who is a self-employed writer and author of several fictional historical romance novels. The Defendant has the financial ability to contribute to the support of the minor children and the Plaintiff."

The issue of custody was also addressed in the statement, "The Plaintiff is a fit and proper person to have custody of the minor children of the parties . . ."

In conclusion, Nancy requested that the Court award her a legal separation, as well as temporary or partial use of the house; joint legal custody of the minor children with shared physical custody; permanent child support and alimony; an equitable share of their property; and counsel fees.

Even as she tried to obtain a legal separation, Nancy

was once again forced to confront the pathological nature of Jeremy's procrastination. Although the four-page legal document was signed by Nancy Linda Richards Akers on February 17, 1999, and delivered to her estranged husband nine days later, Jeremy did not respond to the complaint in a timely fashion. Instead, he waited until the last day before filing a request for additional time to respond. In his motion, which he wrote out in longhand, he stated:

> Defendant Jeremy Ray Akers hereby requests an extension of time of thirty (30) days in which to file a reply to Plaintiff's Complaint. In support thereof, Defendant states that he is the sole provider of day-to-day care for his two young children and that due to the time requirements of that responsibility plus the burdens of sickness and school work, he has been thus far unable to retain the services of an attorney.

In reality, the reasons that Jeremy cited were only a piece of the total picture. Receiving Nancy's official request for a legal separation was like a cold, hard slap in his face. With little hope that his wife would change her mind, Jeremy fell into a depression that made him unable to concentrate on his work. During an afternoon jog with his friend Bill Ranger, he described how his business was suffering due to his inability to concentrate. His friend urged him to pull himself together for the sake of the kids, and get his finances in order. Ranger knew that a judge would never grant Jeremy custody if he could not afford to keep his household running.

Instead, Jeremy obsessed about what might have gone wrong, and convinced himself that menopause was at the root of his wife's irrational behavior. In spite of his frustration at not being able to communicate with her, he continued to allow Nancy access to the children—for a while.

Angered at Jeremy's procrastination in answering her legal complaint, Nancy responded to him through her attorney, filing a Plaintiff's Response and Partial Opposition To Defendant's Motion for Extension of Time. In her two-page filing, she pointed out that Jeremy had waited until the very last day to file his request for more time. She also stated that he was an attorney, explaining to the court that Jeremy's request for an extension of time was, at the least, misleading.

> The children referred to by the Defendant both attend school during the day. Accordingly, it is difficult to understand how the needs of the children during the day seriously impede the Defendant's ability to obtain counsel. In addition, the Defendant is self-employed and his office is in his home. With regard to the sickness of the child or children referred to in the Defendant's Motion, Plaintiff is hard pressed to understand that as a basis for Defendant's Motion, either, since she is not aware that either of the children had any medical treatment during the time in question.

Nancy's attorney urged the court to consider that there were matters of custody and support that needed to be addressed in a timely fashion, and requested that the amount of time given to Jeremy Akers to respond to his client's complaint be shortened to twenty-five days.

But, as the fighting between the couple worsened, Jeremy told Zeb that he did not want his mother visiting the house anymore because her presence was just provoking more fights. Nancy, in turn, accused her estranged husband of poisoning her children's minds against her.

For months, she had tried not to react when Isabelle and

Zeb lashed out at her with harsh criticisms and bitter accusations—fueled and even encouraged, she believed, by Jeremy's undisguised hostility toward her. The children's tirades cut through her like a knife but she hoped that as they got older, they'd understand the circumstances that had forced her to flee from the horror of her life with their father.

She also knew that her leaving was not smiled upon by a society that, feminism notwithstanding, still regarded a woman as the fittest parent. And she knew that she was seen, even by some of her closest friends, as having abandoned her children for the sake of a frivolous affair.

Somehow, she managed to cope with their raised eyebrows and unsubtle, insinuating remarks. But when her kids echoed these sentiments, telling her that she had "left" them, she felt her emotions being tested almost beyond her ability to control them. Her first impulse was always to scream out defensively, telling them that, No, she loved them and would do anything for them, but that if she had stayed in their home, she would have been no good to them or to herself. She would have gone insane!

She never spoke those words, knowing that her children were far too young to fathom the kind of adult problems she and Jeremy were having. At every encounter, however, when eleven-year-old Zeb or ten-year-old Isabelle accused her of "not being there" for them, she ended up biting the inside of her lip, forcing herself to speak to them in calm, reassuring tones.

It was immensely more difficult, however, to hear them echoing Jeremy calling her a tramp and worse. Time after time, she tried to answer their indictments patiently, exhorting them not to use that "bad word" and explaining over and over that she loved them more than she could ever describe.

She was not as controlled with her lawyer, whom she called the second she returned from visiting the children. Babbling into the phone, she regaled Mr. Soschin with lengthy, rambling descriptions of the unfair insults she had endured. But her recapitulations were so long-winded that the lawyer suggested she put her feelings and perceptions into writing—not only to help her deal with her anger but also to spare himself endless hours of listening on the other end of the line.

It was the perfect suggestion for Nancy, who had found emotional redemption and a fair amount of professional success through her writing. What started out as a collection of her thoughts and feelings, anger and frustration, ultimately became a journal rich in introspection and reflection in which she detailed the painful experience of losing her children and the emotions she felt about Jeremy over the course of their tumultuous twenty-year connection.

It seemed a million years had passed since the strapping young lawyer she met through a mutual friend had turned from an object of admiration to one of revulsion and fear. In the beginning, she had been attracted to Jeremy's quick wit and brilliant mind. To her, he was affable, solicitous, charming, a man of strong values who loved children, was a proud patriot, and was especially kind to strangers, the elderly, and single women.

In spite of his diminutive stature, his bulging muscles and resonant, Southern-twanged voice, as well as the politeness and civility that so characterized this gentleman of the deep South made him a formidable presence—not only to Nancy but also to just about every woman he encountered.

Nancy was aware that friends of the dapper former Marine captain were envious of his unerring ability to attract beautiful, interesting, intelligent women. She also appreciated that her "catch" made her the envy of her friends, and she liked that.

But as she grew to know him better, a different Jeremy emerged and her feelings changed. She began to see a man who was opinionated, aggressive, and off-center in his views and attitudes. As time went by, Jeremy's eccentricities grew more pronounced. She was not blind to the knowing looks their friends exchanged when his fiery temper erupted. And it drove her crazy that he was always late and such a chronic procrastinator.

There were times, to be sure, that Nancy's rage melted into pity. She often theorized that his military background had increased Jeremy's innately obsessive nature and that in some perverse way he had transformed the natural disorder of married life and parenthood into a violation of everything for which the Marines stood.

She remembered him telling her tales of his Marine Corps training at the Officer Candidate School in Quantico, Virginia, where he and his fellow officers were drilled relentlessly on the importance of neatness, that cleanliness was next to godliness, and that lateness was a sign of disrespect.

She had listened with fascination to his descriptions of his careful attention to all the sartorial demands of the corps, describing the importance of having his pants neatly pressed so that not one crease was apparent, and of standing in front of the mirror to make sure he looked "perfect." Contrasting this fastidiousness with the slovenly man he had become and the chaotic environment in which he was raising their children evoked sympathy in Nancy, but not enough to negate her rage.

For Nancy, there is no doubt that Jeremy's steadiness of purpose translated into qualities that she had been deprived of in her relationship with her biological father—and perhaps even her adoptive father. "Aha," she may have imagined, "here, finally, is a man who will be as true to me as he is to his other loves—the Marines, the law, physical fitness."

Her journal entries clearly revealed her state of mind and fluctuating moods, which varied from hopeful to despairing, and depended largely upon her weekly visits with Zeb and Isabelle. When she enjoyed a warm and comforting afternoon with them, her notations were infused with optimism. On these days, she drew strength from her attorney's assurances that once a family court judge heard her case, he would rule in her favor and grant her sole or at least joint custody of her two dependent children.

These pronouncements served to quiet the anxiety she felt about the other reality her lawyer had raised: that a judge might very well frown on her voluntary departure from the family home, and the fact that she was living, unmarried, in a one-bedroom basement apartment with another man. It was hardly an appropriate environment for two impressionable preteens.

Nancy was not naïve.

She had no illusions about the uphill nature of her court fight and was painfully aware that her request for custody and child support could be persuasively challenged. But she also believed that once a judge heard her story, and learned of Jeremy's violent tendencies, of the unending taunts, the abusive language, and the death threats, he would see her side.

Sometimes, the fights they had when she visited the children at home would escalate out of control, both of them racing to the phone to summon the police, tripping over each other to tell their side of the story to the uniformed officers of the city's Second District. Yes, the children often witnessed these outbursts, but they had no way of knowing—not at their age, Nancy thought—what they really meant or the kind of devastating toll they had exacted on her mind and spirit. The only thing that seemed to stand between her sanity and madness was the journal in which she faithfully recorded her feelings each night when she returned to her basement apartment.

In an email to a friend, Nancy confided that she moved out of the house to save her life and the lives of her children.

"If I had not left, they might have witnessed my death," she wrote.

Another email to a colleague described Jeremy: "He is a violent, possessive, terrorist control-freak, although I am out of the immediate path of his wrath he has spared nothing in his efforts to punish me financially and emotionally."

Jeremy, meanwhile, continued to refuse help from his family, and ignored their repeated pleas to hire an attorney. Instead, he sought legal advice from his law school friend Don Boswell. During their conversations, he made it clear that his foremost concern was for his children's well-being. Jeremy could not accept the man his wife had chosen as her lover, and that she was parading him around *their* neighborhood for all their friends to see, but he was not concentrating on her or her indiscretion. Instead, he remained focused on what he felt was best for Zeb and Isabelle, and emphasized that he would never permit his children to live under the same roof as Jim—even if a judge granted his wife sole custody. The idea of Jim Lemke playing the role of father figure to his beloved children was utterly unacceptable.

On April 16, 1999, Jeremy responded to Nancy's legal complaint. In a two-page document that he prepared himself, he denied that he and Nancy lived separate and apart within the marital home for several years, and rebuffed

Nancy's claim that they last cohabited as husband and wife in April 1998.

He charged Nancy with abandoning him, the marital home, and their children, and accused her of engaging in "continuous marital misconduct outside the marital home" since approximately August of 1998. He claimed that beginning in January of 1998, Nancy "seriously impaired the physical and emotional well-being of Counterclaimant and her children by engaging in cruel conduct, including, but not limited to, alienation of the children, extreme verbal abuse, insults, threats, physical and emotional intimidation, and assault."

In response to her claims for child and spousal support, Jeremy countered that she was "a successful, self-employed writer and author of a number of fictional romance novels [sic] which have been published by major publishing companies and distributed on both a national and international basis.

"Plaintiff also has a burgeoning business in manufacturing and selling expensive decorative object's art [sic]. The Plaintiff has the financial ability to contribute to the support of all the children as well as the Crossclaimant." Jeremy also pointed out that he had been the sole caregiver for the children since Nancy moved out in August.

In his Counterclaim, Jeremy asked that he be granted a legal separation on the grounds of "cruelty" and that he be given sole custody of the minor children with what he described as "shared physical custody." He also sought child support for Zeb and Isabelle, and spousal support for himself. In addition, he asked the court to legally restrain and enjoin Nancy from alienating the children from him.

Even as the legal battle raged, Finny said that his father remained civilized in his dealings with Nancy. When she asked if she could take the children to Savannah, Georgia, to visit with her mother, he agreed to let them go—so long as she promised that Jim would not accompany her on the journey.

Nancy's attorney said that his client seemed in good spirits and was looking forward to the upcoming court hearing, and the trip to Savannah that would follow. But to her friends, Nancy was painting a very different story, confiding that she was afraid that Jeremy was going to murder her. She recounted a conversation to some friends in which Jeremy told her that he would kill her before he granted her a divorce.

Even as Nancy was claiming that her husband was out to kill her, she continued to visit Zeb and Isabelle at the family home, and even brought her boyfriend and children to an outdoor fair at the children's parochial school.

Members of the parish were aghast when the author turned up at the spring event accompanied by a man who was half her age. Many wondered who this strange man was. Gathering in small groups, they whispered about his casual blue jean attire, the ring that dangled from his earlobe, and the package of cigarettes that was tucked into the sleeve of his shirt. Others raised their eyebrows in recognition of what they suspected was going on, and in tacit condemnation of Nancy. Still others theorized that Nancy was acting out one of the scenarios she had entertained her readers with in her romance novels.

The parents at the school had noticed the clothes that young Isabelle had been wearing since her mother's departure from the family home. Suddenly, the darling little girl who had always been attired in pretty dresses was out in public wearing halters and tube tops that showed off her bare belly, and tight stretch pants that they thought were inappropriate. Her long blonde hair always appeared to be in need of a brushing, and her infectious smile had been replaced by a sullen expression.

In part, Zeb and Isabelle were upset that their mother kept on promising them that she would come over to their house to make them dinner, but then cancel at the last minute in teary phone calls. "I can't come over tonight," Nancy explained between sobs. "But I can't tell you why I can't come."

On April 27, 1999, a little more than one month before her murder, Nancy answered Jeremy's Counterclaim. She denied her husband's allegations of abandonment, but admitted that since August of 1998, she had lived separate and apart from her husband and children in a one-bedroom apartment also occupied by James Lemke.

In addressing Jeremy's accusation of "continuous marital misconduct," she stated that she could not deny or admit the claim since she did not understand what he meant by the term. But she disputed Jeremy's assertion that her actions had seriously impaired the physical and emotional well-being of him and the children, and denied his allegations of abuse. While she acknowledged that several of her books had been published and distributed both nationally and internationally, and that she had recently taken up selling art objects, she refuted Jeremy's claim that she was financially successful and independent. To the contrary, she stated that her gross income for 1998 from all of her business endeavors was $10,202.00, and that her net income was $1,913.00.

Finally, she rebuffed Jeremy's claim that he had been taking sole care of Zeb and Isabelle since her departure in August, and further disputed his request for sole custody of the children. In closing, she asked the court to dismiss her husband's counterclaim and grant her a legal separation based on her complaint.

In May, Nancy's best friend hosted a party for her at her home near Georgetown. She wanted to give her an opportunity to showcase her evening bags and jewelry, and to earn the extra income that she so desperately needed. When Nancy arrived to set up her bags for the show, Emily could not help but notice that her friend had put on a lot of weight and was now close to two hundred pounds. Then Emily observed her helping herself to a Coke—something that she never would have done in the past. The two women had spent months on a strict exercise and diet regimen and always drank diet soda.

"You're drinking soda with sugar in it?" Emily inquired, noting that her friend's face was bloated. "We always drank diet soda."

"Not anymore," Nancy responded matter-of-factly.

Nancy broke down in tears when her friend suggested that they go back on their diet. "I haven't gained any weight," she insisted as she fought to control her emotions, and to conceal her anger that Emily had insinuated that she looked heavy.

Other friends of the couple began to wonder if something was amiss at the Akers home. They had often called to chat with Nancy or Jeremy, but their calls went unanswered.

Kathleen Karr recalled that a message she left for Nancy in April went unanswered. Jeremy's childhood pal, Ray Walker, suspected that something wasn't right when Jerry did not return the message that he left for him on the answering machine. One of the last times that Ray had visited with his elementary school chum was in 1996, when he and his wife had come to the District on holiday. It was during that visit that Ray was first introduced to Nancy and the couple's three children. Ray recalled being surprised by the woman Jeremy had chosen to be his wife. With her hair slicked back neatly in a bun, and no makeup adorning her face, the buxom brunette was worlds apart from the slight "cheerleader-types" Jeremy had dated through high school and college.

Another thing that surprised Ray was Jerry's knack for caring for his children. One afternoon, the former Marine showed up to take him and his wife on a tour of the city with Zeb and Isabelle in tow. Watching how patient and caring Jerry was with the youngsters seemed out of character for the man he had known for so many years.

Ray and Jeremy would call each other from time to time, never on any particular schedule, but when they had a moment to break away from their work. As days turned to weeks and weeks turned to months, Ray began to wonder what was going on with his friend. But he continued to think that Jerry would return his call at some point.

Jeremy even seemed to be trying to hide the truth from people he talked to regularly. His friend Tom Turchin would later tell a reporter that he had had several conversations with Jeremy over the months and his friend never mentioned that his wife had moved in with another man.

Near the end of May, Avery Drake, the young boy who had lived next door to the Akerses on 44th Avenue, spotted Nancy crossing MacArthur Boulevard with her children. Nancy had put on quite a bit of weight since Avery last saw her, but he recognized the kids almost instantly. He had often spent time with Zeb and Isabelle and their father at the park just up the street. Over the last few years, Jeremy had become a regular in their pick-up basketball games, and frequently spent time playing Frisbee with his kids, and romping with the family dogs.

But Nancy had a new man on her arm, someone Avery had never seen with either Nancy or the kids. He wondered who this person was, and what had happened to Jeremy. A few days later, he saw the young man again, this time as he and Nancy walked in the front door of the liquor store where he worked.

Unbeknownst to him, the couple lived in the apartment building right across from the store on MacArthur Boulevard. He watched as Nancy and her companion browsed the aisles, picking up a six-pack of beer and some inexpensive wine.

But Drake would not learn who Jim was until several weeks later when he picked up *The Washington Post* and read the front-page headline about Nancy's murder.

CHAPTER THIRTEEN

By 6 P.M., THE TEMPERATURE OUTSIDE HAD DROPPED from a sweltering eighty-eight to a balmy sixty-four degrees. A thin, low-lying layer of clouds moved slowly across the sky as Nancy Richards Akers nervously waited in the living room of the Washington, DC brownstone which only months earlier she had called her home.

It was Saturday, the fifth of June, and Nancy was counting the minutes until her two youngest children bounded down the staircase and—she hoped—greeted her with the hugs and kisses she had missed so much over the past ten months. It was startling, even to her, that so much time had elapsed since she had escaped from her stultifying marriage to Jeremy and moved into a basement apartment with her young lover.

But the price had been high.

Nearly a month had passed since her last journal entry on May 10th. While anguish and anger usually inspired her writing, calmer times allowed the tireless novelist a welcome break in her non-stop entries. But the weeks leading up to June 5 had been filled with a special kind of torture for Nancy, leaving friends to imagine that the blank pages of her journal may have meant that she was too depressed to continue writing.

One friend recalled Nancy telling her that on some nights she was so exhausted that she threw on her nightgown, smeared some toothpaste over her teeth, looked at her wearied image in the mirror and fell into bed. But instead of falling asleep, she would find her mind teeming with snapshots of the day and with exploding thoughts of rage, frustration, and worry.

Starting in mid-May, Jeremy had begun a three-week campaign of new tortures for Nancy. Yet, no record of them can be found in her journal, leaving only her friends to describe what transpired during this most difficult time in Nancy's life. Finny, her attorney, and her friends all painted very different pictures about Nancy's relationship with Jeremy in the final weeks.

Finny recalled that his parents seemed to be getting along reasonably well until the day that Jeremy caught Nancy rifling through his office papers. Outraged, and convinced that she was looking for information to use against him in their upcoming custody battle, he forbade her from coming to the house when he was not there, and changed all the locks on the doors.

Nancy's attorney said that he did not sense that anything was out of the ordinary. Beginning in early April, Alan Soschin noticed that his client had shifted her focus away from the day-to-day squabbles with Jeremy about their kids, and was concentrating on the legal details of her separation. She did not express any concern or fear for her safety. Instead, he recalled that she was looking forward to the upcoming mediation hearing and was curious to see how Jeremy would react before the mediator.

But one of Nancy's friends contends that Jeremy was torturing her emotionally, refusing to take her calls and forbidding her to see the children. She even witnessed Jeremy's increasingly odd behavior first-hand when he showed up at her home to pick up Zeb and Isabelle. When she answered the door, she said that Jeremy questioned her aggressively about Nancy, asking how often she visited, and angrily accusing her of entertaining Nancy in her home with Jim by her side. The woman explained that she cared about both Jeremy and Nancy, but wasn't going to get in the middle of their marital problems. When he continued to confront her, she let him know that she did not like his tone and she told him to back off. Immediately, Jeremy shrank back and apologized.

By some accounts, Jeremy's behavior seemed to worsen as the court date approached. Nancy's friend remembers hearing from a mutual acquaintance about an incident in which Jeremy had harassed her while she was out for a stroll. The woman recounted how he had raced up to her on the sidewalk, and accused her of conspiring with Nancy and her friends to ridicule him behind his back. Standing just inches away from her, he ranted on about how Nancy and her friends were probably all getting together on a regular basis to talk about him, and laughing about what a loser he was. The woman grew scared at Jeremy's paranoid thinking and listened as he continued to carry on about the imaginary meetings. Eventually, she was able to break away from him and run home.

It was clear even to Jeremy's closest friends that the battle-hardened Vietnam veteran was coming apart at the seams. His business in shambles, Jeremy was losing his means of financial support. Worse yet, it was slowly becoming clear to him that Nancy was not coming back to him—ever. His children were all he had left, and he seemed to be on the verge of losing them, too.

Even Nancy sensed that he was a man on the edge. Weeks before the murder, she again confided in a friend that Jeremy had vowed that he would kill her before he granted her a divorce. Yet, she expressed her continued belief that her children were in no danger and continued to allow them to live in the custody of a man whom she said had verbalized murder threats.

Nancy told her friends that it was hard for her to believe that the man she had married, the man she had chased in hot pursuit clear across the country, the man with whom she had raised three children, had mutated into such a monster.

Nancy was sad and furious but also, ironically, hopeful. Her court date for a mediation hearing was scheduled for June 17, and she knew she'd only have to endure the next few weeks before the way would be paved for a speedy resolution to her custody fight. Surely, she reasoned, Jeremy's recent behavior would tilt the judge's decision in her favor.

Meanwhile, her attorney was advising her that she needed to find a different address in order to present an appearance of stability and reliability. He worried that a judge would not look favorably on her request for custody as long as she was sharing a one-bedroom apartment with a boyfriend. But she was not earning enough money to pay for an apartment of her own, and she was not prepared to ask her friends for help. Not only did she fear that her friends would be worried about the possible threat Jeremy might pose; she was also conflicted about acting in a way that did not include Jim. Her attempts at finding her own place consisted of compiling a list with a friend of acquaintances who might have a guest wing or housekeepers' quarters she could use.

Nancy's need for extra income prompted her to make plans to peddle her handbags and other crafts at the outdoor community market scheduled for Saturday, June 5. She had designed many of the evening bags in her collection herself, staying up nights to painstakingly affix the sparkly sequins and colorful beads to the elegant silk and satin purses.

Weather forecasters had predicted a perfect day for the outdoor market, with temperatures reaching into the high eighties. Yet, in spite of the ideal weather conditions, all the friends she had invited to the event told her that they were unable to clear their schedules to attend.

Just the night before, in response to an inquiry she had received, Nancy had emailed fellow author Kathy Seidel, who wanted to know more about the handcrafted purses, to suggest that Kathy stop by and view some of her latest creations. Kathy had learned of Nancy's personal difficulties from Mary Kilchenstein, who was worried about their mutual friend and urged the writers who knew her to help her out by buying one of her bags.

> *From: Nancy*
> *To: Kathy*
> *Date: Friday, June 04, 1999 4:54 PM*
> *Subject: Re:*
>
> *Kathy,*
> *I would love to show the bags to you . . . No, you're not a visual idiot. Photos are so hard to judge even under the best of circumstances, and one never knows how things pop up in different browsers . . . I don't know how much Mary told you of my situation, but I do not live at home anymore and have been unable to afford my own housing, so I am 'guest' in the apartment of a young man on MacArthur Boulevard . . . he has been extremely gracious and patient, especially when I started painting and occupying more space. Anyway, it would be best if I brought some things to you since I hate to impose any more than I already am.*
>
> *Let me know what kind of date and time would*

work best for you, and I will be there. Byeeee for
now, Nancy.

For a moment, Kathy contemplated stopping by Nancy's
booth that afternoon. The craft market was being held less
than five minutes from her home, and she tried to rearrange
her busy Saturday schedule to squeeze the show in. But, at
the last minute she decided against it because she had a
long list full of errands to run. Besides, she thought, there
was no real urgency. She could have Nancy over to her
house later that week, not only to look at the bags but also
to catch up on things.

Their meeting was never to be.

Early on the morning of June 5, Nancy stood in the
living room of her cramped apartment and carefully placed
the last of her crafts into a satchel. As she reached for the
apartment door, one friend recalled, she heard the telephone
ring. Grabbing the receiver, she was surprised to hear Jeremy inviting her to come over to the house to take the kids
to dinner at McDonald's that evening. While she considered
the phone call bizarre, she was eager to concentrate more
on his willingness to let her visit the children without a
hassle than on the apparent change in his personality. She
chose to interpret the call as a sign that he was coming
around and that their court date, in just twelve days, would
be at least amicable.

"I'll be there around six to pick them up," Nancy told
him.

Rejuvenated by Jeremy's unexpected—and benevolently
proffered—invitation, she grabbed her tote bag of crafts,
locked the apartment door behind her, and headed for the
outdoor market. But another of Nancy's friends insists that
Jeremy's invitation to take the children to dinner did not
come in the form of a phone call. Instead, she says the

invitation was extended in-person when he and the kids made an unexpected stop by the booth Nancy was renting to sell her wares.

Arriving back at the one-bedroom flat later that afternoon, Nancy quickly readied herself for her dinner outing with Zeb and Isabelle. Reaching into her dresser drawer, she pulled out the size extra-large navy-and-white–striped sleeveless T-shirt that she would wear with a pair of black, elastic-waistband slacks. In less than two years, the forty-eight-year-old mother had gone from wearing sexy, figure-revealing outfits to baggy, oversized clothes. At 194 pounds, the five-foot, four-inch author was pained, she confided to a friend, to be mistaken on more than one occasion for a woman who was pregnant and about to give birth. Yet, in spite of her large size, she continued to buy delicate, Victoria's Secret bra-and-panty ensembles.

She glanced down at her toenails, each one painted a different color, as she slipped her feet into the comfortable Josef Seidel shoes she so loved. Hurrying into the living room, Nancy grabbed her hunter-green Coach pocketbook from the sofa.

Turning to Jim, who was sprawled out on the couch, she asked, "Can I bring you back anything from McDonald's?"

"A strawberry shake," he answered.

"Okay." Nancy smiled, blowing her lover a kiss as she closed the apartment door behind her for the last time.

When she arrived to pick up the children, Jeremy greeted her with cool politeness. Some friends say she remained outside in the Jeep and waited for the kids to emerge, as she had been instructed by her attorney, while others insist she went inside to greet her children in person.

"I'm here!" she called up to Zeb and Isabelle from the

bottom of the staircase, heartened by their cheery "Be right there, Mom" response.

As she waited, Nancy's dark eyes scanned the familiar surroundings. Papers littered the couches, tables, chairs, and floor. Some were piled so high that she could barely see the blue-and-white porcelain dishes and framed family photographs that accented the room. It was not as if she had been the most meticulous housekeeper—far from it, she acknowledged to herself with a twinge of guilt—but this was an environment that was patently out of control. There were stacks of old newspapers dating back more than eight months, and suitcases by the front door that had still not been unpacked from Jeremy's business travels several months earlier.

She remembered her own manuscripts strewn here and there as she tried to juggle the demands of three active kids with the non-negotiable deadlines of her editors. She felt more than a pang of envy thinking about the maids who cleaned her mother's home but not her own, thanks to the shortage of money she and Jeremy always seemed to struggle with. Now, the sty-like mess that encircled her eclipsed any shortcomings she believed she had in the domestic area.

Passing from the living room that she had so thoughtfully decorated with collectibles and antiques to the home's tiny kitchen, she could feel her stomach tightening. She viewed the empty egg cartons, stacks of old newspapers, and assorted junk randomly strewn on the countertops, the dishes piled in the sink, and the garbage pail in the corner that was brimming with crusty food containers and assorted household trash. An overwhelming sense of guilt and fury washed over her because her decision to leave the house had relegated her children to living in such a dirty, disorderly environment.

Nancy heaved a deep sigh of resignation and turned to

leave the cramped galley-style kitchen. The thought of making the place livable was replaced by her anger at Jeremy and the compulsive pack-rat habits of the man that she was once proud of to call her husband. She had never understood his overwhelming compulsion to collect and hold on to every insignificant thing, including meaningless items from their neighbors' trash bins.

Her irritation at his inability to throw anything away was rivaled only by her frustration with the maddening excuse he gave her about how they might someday need this or that article. What, she had wondered a thousand times over the years, would they ever do with the mountains of old newspapers and the dozens of brochures, applications, and IRS forms that Jeremy felt compelled to save?

Scanning the untidiness, she resolved once again to write down her observations in the electronic journal she kept on her computer in the hope they would help her in the impending custody battle. Her entries had helped her to clarify her thoughts and feelings in the four months that she had been recording all of the complexities of her life; they would now help, she was certain, with her court case.

Thinking about all this left a bitter taste in her mouth, but as she cast her eyes toward the entranceway, she smiled at the sight of the old wire mannequin that stood ever at the ready to greet visitors. The antique dressmaker's form had always been her favorite element of the decor.

All at once, Nancy's meandering ruminations were interrupted by the sound of clattering footsteps as Zeb and Isabelle bounded down the stairs and jumped, one at a time, from the third step onto the center hall's hardwood floor, greeting her with uncharacteristic exuberance.

Nancy knew that her children's emotions had been buffeted back and forth and high and low by an angry but devoted father and a loving but absent mother. While Isabelle seemed to have weathered the trauma in her life with an admirable degree of equanimity, Zeb hadn't had it so easy. He was angry with his mother and rarely let her forget her transgressions, leveling charges of abandonment and bad mothering at her during most of her visits. He echoed his father's charges of bad character and loose morals whenever he had the opportunity.

Yet on this occasion, both children seemed loving and receptive to Nancy's visit. She wondered why for a brief second. That quickly evaporated as she soaked up their enthusiastic greetings.

"Hi, Mommy!" Isabelle chirped, her long blonde hair flying behind her.

"Hiya, Mom," Zeb intoned in a more serious voice, but with an irresistibly attractive grin on his face.

Nancy, suddenly overcome by emotion, choked back tears as she ran to hug her children.

"So, what'll it be?" she asked them, recovering her composure to affect a mock-serious tone. "Some tuna fish sandwiches?"

"No!" they cried in unison. "McDonald's!"

Leading the way down the brick walkway, Zeb grabbed the handle of his mother's shiny red Jeep Wrangler, a car that was registered to Jim Lemke's mother in Chicago. Trailing behind him and Isabelle, Nancy felt the weight of the world melt away as she breathed the warm late-afternoon air. She caught sight of the German Embassy across the road, its mustard-yellow façade and angular, modern design partially hidden by towering evergreen trees. For years, she had enjoyed looking at the sprawling compound, noting with satisfaction that it lent a great deal of prestige to her own home. She climbed into her car, turned on the ignition, checked that her kids had put on their seat belts, and drove off, noting that the clock on the dash registered 6:15 p.m.

Friends have speculated that it it must have been a pleasant evening for Nancy and her children or the children would have insisted on going home early. Instead, the evening lasted four hours.

Other friends disagree. They believed that there was so much tension between Nancy and her children that their last evening together could well have been filled with conflict and even tears. The children were very angry with their mother, unable to believe that she had abandoned them— and that she was blind to how much her actions hurt their father.

At the end of the evening, Nancy drove Zeb and Isabelle back home, arriving a little before 10 p.m. She kissed them both goodbye, remaining in the driver's seat as she watched them walk the few steps to the porch.

When they had gone about halfway, she saw Jeremy open the front door. With purposeful steps, he strode toward her car.

When they had gone about halfway, she saw Jeremy open the front door. He was dressed in jeans and a pullover, even though the temperature was in the seventies and the humidity was high. With purposeful steps, he strode toward her car.

"Nancy," he began brusquely, "we need to talk."

Jerking open the Jeep's door, he leaned forward, his face close to hers. "It's time for you to come to your senses," he insisted. "I want you to come back home."

"No," she returned, making it clear there was nothing he could do to change her mind.

The emotional intensity of the conversation quickly escalated. Jeremy's deep, throaty voice was thick with anger as he continued to demand that she return home. Nancy resisted, saying no over and over again. She shook her head hard, keeping her eyes fixed straight ahead and refusing to look at him.

Their voices got louder, echoing in the darkness of the night. The children, who had paused on the front walk, were paralyzed by the scene developing before them. They could now hear pieces of the argument, and grew increasingly alarmed when it began to focus on them.

Their eyes remained fixed on their parents, two silhouettes barely visible under the darkened sky, as they saw their father reach behind him deliberately. While Isabelle's view was partially blocked by the large tree sprouting in the middle of the front lawn, young Zeb had an unfettered view from the front portico.

Suddenly a new sound, something even more terrifying, cut through the stillness of the night. The two shots of the .380-caliber pistol sounded like the popping of firecrackers.

Isabelle immediately turned and ran inside the house.

It was only a matter of seconds before her father ran up the walkway and into the house after her. "Call somebody," he instructed her cooly.

The little girl stood frozen as she watched her father grab a bulky object that was wrapped in the family's blue-and-white–checkered tablecloth and race back down the slate walkway toward his SUV.

"We love you, Daddy!" Isabelle and Zeb shouted after him from the portico as they watched their father dash off, tears streaming down their faces.

Running back inside the house, Isabelle picked up the telephone receiver and dialed her eighty-year-old grandparents in Sheffield, Alabama.

"Granny Akers, it's Isabelle." The little girl's voice remained steady. "Daddy just shot Mommy in the head and drove away."

Granny Akers, amazingly keeping her composure, told her ten-year-old granddaughter to hang up immediately and call 911.

Handing the telephone to her brother, the slender child with the wavy blonde hair calmly explained that Granny had instructed her to hang up and call for help.

Zeb, taking control, dialed 911, and spoke with uncanny coherence to the operator.

"911, where's your emergency?" the operator inquired. "What's wrong?"

"My mother was shot," the young boy said into the receiver.

"Shot?" the operator inquired.

"Yes, sir," Zeb answered, echoing the language he had heard from his military father.

"With a gun?" The operator was puzzled.

"Yes." Zeb's voice cracked as he tried to fight back tears.

"Okay. Where was she shot at? Take it easy. We'll bring you some help."

"Okay . . ."

"All right, I'm sending you some help, okay? Whoever shot her, are they still there?"

"No."

As the eleven-year-old related the unbelievable scenario that had just taken place, his mother lay lifeless in the red Jeep Wrangler, her body splayed out in bloody horror on the front seat of the car.

CHAPTER FOURTEEN

At about 10:40 p.m., roughly forty minutes after Jeremy Akers shot his wife, Sergeant Michael Farish ordered one of his uniformed officers to stand guard outside the house to secure the crime scene, and allow the department to obtain a search warrant for the premises. The protective sweep of the stately residence had turned up clean, with the officers finding no trace of Jeremy, any hostages, or any additional victims.

Acting under Farish's orders, the officers began a methodical search of the neighborhood, looking and listening for any indication that the perpetrator was still in the area. Officers fanned out along the street, using the narrow beams of their flashlights to check behind bushes and houses. Others rang doorbells, hoping to find a neighbor who had witnessed the crime. Some of the officers recalled having been summoned to the Akers home on previous occasions because of fights between Jeremy and his wife over the kids.

One woman told police that she had seen Jeremy sitting on the stoop in front of his house earlier that evening, drinking from a bottle of Jack Daniel's. Another reported that he had seen Jeremy talking to Nancy as she sat in her Jeep. A third person remembered seeing Jeremy driving away in his Mercury Mountaineer. And several neighbors told police that they knew that the Akerses were going through a divorce and, on occasion, had overheard arguments between the two.

The arrival of additional unmarked vehicles on the scene created a flurry of excitement among members of the local press corps, who crowded behind the crime scene tape. Furiously, they began scribbling on their notepads as three members of top-level police brass climbed out of the cars.

Sergeant Farish also focused his attention on the newcomers. He instantly recognized "the nighthawk," Ross Swope, who was in uniform and, as acting chief of the department, was responsible for overseeing the crime scene when the Chief of Police was off-duty. District Commander Shannon Cockett was there too, in uniform. But Farish did not know the third man in plainclothes who was also demanding answers from him.

"And you are . . . ?" the sergeant asked.

Farish's question caught the commander by surprise. "Gene Marlin, field operations commander," he said. Relatively new to the department, Marlin was the commander in charge of "the nighthawks" and was Swope's boss.

Farish nodded. Even in a city with one of the highest murder rates in the nation, there was no question in the sergeant's mind as to why this particular homicide scene was drawing so much attention from police brass. Directly across the street at the German Embassy, guards now stood poised with machine guns in front of wooden barricades. The brass knew this case was going to be getting more than its share of ink from the media, and they wanted to make sure that the investigation was being properly conducted.

Farish was confident that he had covered all the bases. The three detectives on the scene—Dwayne Partman, Ralph Durant, and Dejuan Williams—were busy at work. He had assigned an officer to accompany Nancy Akers' body to the emergency room. He also had directed his men to canvass the neighborhood, keeping on top of their activities on a minute-by-minute basis, maintaining regular communica-

tion with them via the department's "talk-around" channel.
The system allowed him to talk to officers who were within
a few blocks' radius while the dispatcher was on the line.

As Farish responded to questions from the three commanders, he noticed that David Eyster was among the officers on duty that night and was immediately heartened by
his presence. Until recently, Eyster had been an officer assigned to the Youth Division, working with traumatized
children and young adults. He had just been promoted to
sergeant and was assigned to the Second District—Farish's
district—as a patrol sergeant. Farish had confidence that
Eyster would be of great assistance in his next task: interviewing the Akers children, who were the only witnesses
to the shooting.

After Eyster had been apprised of the situation, he accompanied Farish into the home of the Akerses' next-door
neighbor. Passing through the living room, the officer noted
the presence of several small children, including a newborn
baby. They found both Zeb and Isabelle sitting numbly on
a couch in the family room.

While both men were braced for an emotional outpour-
ing from the children of the murdered and the murderer,
they found instead two preteens sitting upright, and in Farish's words, "calm, collected, composed, and mannerly."

Farish knew that interviewing children who had just
been involved in a horrific incident was always a challenge—and that the interviewer had to be careful not to
"hit the button" that would trigger hysterics. His immediate
goal was to find out what had happened, and if, in fact, it
was their father who had shot their mother.

His approach was to ask a series of low-key questions
that would elicit the answers he was looking for. Because
Eyster had considerably more experience in this area, Farish let him lead the questioning.

Sergeant Eyster decided to direct his questions at Zeb, who seemed unusually composed, and from the outset of the investigation precociously intelligent. At first, Zeb's answers gave little information to the seasoned investigator. At one point, the eleven-year-old responded to a question by saying: "I am sorry, that would be more beneficial to you if I were to answer than to my father." Most other questions, however, were answered with a simple, "Yes, sir" or "No, sir."

Yet Zeb and Isabelle were not always so dispassionate. It became clear to Farish that Zeb was angry with his mother—and that Jeremy had been fueling the flames. It also became obvious to him that Jeremy had told the children that their mother was a whore and that their mother and Jim were "touching each other in inappropriate places." Zeb was as protective of his father as he was furious with his mother for abandoning him and his sister.

Zeb also told the police that his older brother was in Kill Devil Hills. Farish was familiar with the place as the site of the Wright Brothers' first flight, and he knew it was on the Outer Banks area of North Carolina. Zeb provided the officers with Finny's phone number, as well as the number of his grandparents in Alabama.

The fact that Finny was "of age" made him the obvious choice as temporary custodian of the younger children. Farish stepped into the hall to call him. After Finny heard the bare-bones details he immediately jumped into a car with his girlfriend and began the trip north to Washington. The children's grandmother in Alabama was also notified, as was the Department of Social Services, which took temporary custody of the children until Finny's arrival. But in all the commotion, no one from Nancy's family was contacted.

Still in the family room of the neighbor's residence, Farish and Eyster tried to learn the address of Nancy's boy-friend. They were convinced that the blind rage of Jeremy Akers would make Jim Lemke his next victim. But while the children told Farish the phone number of Nancy's best friend, Emily, the only information they had about Lemke was his general location.

Leaving Eyster with the children, Farish strode briskly to his car, and dialed Emily's number on his cell phone. He hoped that she could provide him with the information necessary to prevent another violent crime.

Emily picked up the phone on the first ring, still groggy from a deep sleep. When Farish told her what had hap-pened, she was stunned. After regaining her composure, she immediately volunteered to come right down to be with the children. But Farish warned her to stay home, lock all her doors and windows, and keep all the lights off in case Jer-emy came looking for her. When she continued to insist on "being there" for the children, Farish told her that the most helpful thing she could do was supply him with Jim Lemke's phone number, which she did.

He immediately dispatched several officers to the area, hoping it was not too late. His next step was dialing Jim's number to alert him to the fact that he was in danger. As Farish pressed the numbers on the keypad, he was com-pletely unaware that at that very moment, the fugitive he was looking for was less than one mile away from him, skulking around the back alley of 4840 MacArthur Boule-vard in search of his next intended victim.

Crouching behind the garbage pails that obstructed the view of basement apartment T-R2, Jeremy kicked at the iron grating that safeguarded the above-ground windows, mind-ful not to wake the neighbors or call attention to himself. His keen sense of feeling out the enemy, honed during his years as an officer of the most prestigious branch of the United States military, told him that his victim was cowering inside, crouching in a corner of the darkened apartment. Peering through the smog-streaked glass panes, he strained to get a good look inside the cramped living area. A sick feeling crept over him as he caught sight of the desk that had once been the centerpiece of his wife's first-floor office.

Realizing that he could not gain entrance through the ground-level windows, Jeremy went around to the front of the five-story apartment building. His heart pumped furiously as he scanned the names and numbers on the building's glass-encased directory.

His rage escalated as he began ringing the buzzer to apartment T-R2. It was clear to him that Jim had to pay for his sins in the same way Nancy had. Pure logic dictated that the man who had stolen his wife and disgraced him in front of his children, his friends, and everyone else who knew him deserved to be punished, and punished in the most pernicious way. If the destruction of his life hadn't been enough, Jeremy felt, then the low-life who continued to flaunt what he had done by moving into a seedy, one-bedroom flat with Nancy, on the very same street where Jeremy and his children lived, was more than enough reason to do away with him. He was the enemy, and if there was one thing Jeremy knew better than most people, the enemy had to be destroyed.

"Lemke, I know you're in there!" Jeremy growled in the direction of the building's intercom, his deep, throaty voice echoing in the darkness. "Come on out. I want to talk to you!"

The silence told Jeremy that either Lemke wasn't home—or that he wasn't coming out. He also realized that he was running out of time. There was no doubt in his mind that by this point, the police were already on his tail.

But Jeremy Akers had absolutely no intention of being taken alive.

As Jeremy steered his Mercury Mountaineer toward the Rock Creek Parkway, his emotions ran the gamut from fits of burning rage to spasms of regret—not for what he had done, but for what he had failed to do. That Nancy had left him for another man—a much younger and less educated man—was a dishonor of the highest order. His only disappointment was that he hadn't killed *him* too! He had hoped to find them together, to make Nancy and her lover pay for their sin at the same time.

He was ten times the man Lemke was, Jeremy thought bitterly. Even now, at the age of fifty-seven, he could still outplay men half his age at basketball, jog more than ten miles a day, and sport a physique that he knew was the envy of men decades younger than himself.

As he maneuvered his powerful SUV along the winding parkway, passing Washington landmarks like the Watergate Hotel and the Kennedy Center, Jeremy continued to recount his assets—assets that Nancy had clearly forgotten about, he fumed, when she decided to abandon her family for some cheap thrills.

It wasn't enough that he had graduated from the University of Virginia's prestigious School of Law, and received a Silver Star, two Purple Hearts, and countless other medals and honors, including a citation from the President of the United States, for his service in the Marines during the Vietnam War. And it wasn't enough for her, he fumed, that he had served as an assistant state attorney in Dade County under the direction of Janet Reno and was also counsel for the United States Justice Department. That he had worked as counsel to numerous companies on Superfund site-related problems, spending weeks, sometimes months, in hotels to further his career, and provide for his family.

No, nothing had been enough for Nancy's outsized ambitions, he concluded angrily, for her constant status-seeking and her chronic, oppressive discontent.

The final straw for Jeremy, it would become clear, was Nancy's intention of taking his children away from him. The thought of Jim Lemke even trying to fill his shoes sickened and enraged him.

His ruminations had escalated to a furious pitch by the time the Memorial Bridge came into sight. With his destination already in mind, Jeremy veered off to the left, heading onto Constitution Avenue. As he spotted a parking space, he stepped hard on the brake and pulled in. He picked up the bundle wrapped in the blue-and-white–checkered tablecloth that he had carefully placed next to him on the front seat. Cradling it gingerly in his arms, he strode toward the National Mall—the home of the Vietnam Veterans Memorial, with the names of many of the fallen heroes he had fought alongside engraved in granite.

Yet he didn't go directly to the mournful black monument. Instead, he continued past the Lincoln Memorial, stopping at one of two freestanding pay phones that lined the walkway to call his old buddy, Bill Ranger.

"He's a trained killer, a hunter who grew up in a rural area in the South, a guy at home in the woods, a man who knows weapons," Sergeant Farish told the three commanders as they stood on the lawn outside Jeremy Akers' house. "I am not sending my guys out with a flashlight to run through the woods with Rambo."

The police officials on the scene were considering mobilizing a manhunt, sending officers into a nearby park where Jeremy frequently hiked with Zeb and Isabelle. But Farish didn't like this strategy, convinced that his men had not been properly trained for an action that, to him, amounted to jungle warfare.

Many of the officers, he knew, were city folk, raised in urban centers like Philadelphia and downtown DC. Even the idea of an overhead search, conducted by a helicopter equipped with infrared lights, didn't make the idea of a full-out manhunt any more palatable. Besides, he knew that there was a pecking order when it came to using the helicopter. The United States Park Police had first dibs, then the Medevacs, and finally the Metropolitan Police Department.

He and his men continued to go back and forth with possible solutions to the problem of finding enough resources for a full-scale effort when one of his officers tapped him on the shoulder.

"There's somebody here you'll want to talk to," the stocky officer whispered in the Sergeant's ear.

Farish followed him down to the barricade the police had constructed and was introduced to a friend of Jeremy Akers who reported that he had just received a phone call from the alleged murderer.

Farish was relieved that Bill Ranger had brought something even more important than the news of the phone call: the phone number from which the call had been made.

Learning that Jeremy had left a large part of his rambling message on Ranger's machine, the sergeant instructed one of his officers to accompany Ranger back to his home to hear the tape.

Meanwhile, Farish pulled out his cell phone and dialed the number that Ranger had provided to him. Impatiently, he listened to it ring repeatedly. He was about to hang up when he heard a man's voice on the other end.

"Who's this?" Farish demanded.

"Who's *this*?" the voice repeated.

Farish's mind raced. It sounded to him as if the man who had answered the phone was out of breath, and he was not sure if he had dialed a cell phone or a pay phone, or if he had reached Jim Lemke, Jeremy Akers, or someone else.

The two men went back and forth, neither wanting to reveal who he was. Finally, Farish identified himself as a member of the Metropolitan Police Department. In turn, he learned that the person who had answered the phone was Sergeant Vincent Guadioso of the United States Park Police.

"Where are you?" Farish asked.

"The pay phone by the Lincoln Memorial," the officer replied.

The horrifying scenario that was about to unfold immediately became clear in Farish's mind. He realized that the suspicion that had haunted him—that Akers was going to head for one of the Washington's war memorials—had been right on. The Lincoln Memorial was located near three such sites, one of them the famous Vietnam War memorial, commonly known as "The Wall."

Something else also became clear—that Guadioso's men were in danger.

"You tell your guys to be careful," Farish warned his fellow officer, after summarizing the events of the evening. "This guy has made it clear he has no intention of being taken alive."

CHAPTER FIFTEEN

EVEN BEFORE FARISH'S PHONE CALL, GUADIOSO HAD been alerted to the fact that there was a man with a gun on the loose.

"Man with gun!" the disembodied voice had crackled over the radio strapped to Guadioso's shoulder about twenty minutes earlier. The veteran officer scanned the darkness for signs of movement. "We have a description of the suspect," the announcement continued. "Male . . . wearing a dark-colored sweatshirt, and blue jeans. Last seen driving a Mercury Mountaineer with Alabama tags . . . suspect possibly armed with a handgun."

Guadioso had been in the vicinity of the Lincoln Memorial Circle when the call blared over his two-way radio. Jumping on his Honda motorcycle, he checked his watch. It read 00:26 hours, 12:26 a.m. civilian time. Keying the mike, he responded to the broadcast.

"Roger," he announced. "I'm on the lookout."

It was Sunday, the sixth of June 1999, and the thirty-seven-year-old Guadioso, a "beat" officer, had been assigned to night patrol of the Lincoln Memorial, one of the more popular tourist attractions in the District of Columbia's vast National Park system. In spite of the patchy clouds wafting overhead, the temperature was a pleasant sixty-four degrees and the uniformed sergeant had elected to ride on one of the department's 250cc Yamaha motor scooters—a benefit reserved for officers with motorcycle training.

Instinctively, he surveyed the people strolling in front of the Greek architecture that houses Abraham Lincoln's marble likeness, searching their expressions for anything out of the ordinary. His pale blue eyes continued to dart around the perimeter of the traffic circle as he slowed his navy-blue motor scooter and directed it toward the curb to wait for more information.

As he scanned the area for anything suspicious, the dispatcher's voice crackled once again over the radio receiver, broadcasting that the suspect had made a telephone call that police had traced to a pay phone on French Drive, just a few yards away from where the sergeant was now stationed.

Dropping the Yamaha into gear, he steered his scooter up onto the cement pavement, rounded the deserted tourist shanty, and headed for the two freestanding pay phones that bordered the walkway. The balmy night air sprayed his windshield with mist as he drove in closer to the suspect's supposed location, his heart beating faster as he neared the two telephones. As the mild evening's breeze blew against his face, his heart began to race. Nearing the phones in a mad dash to investigate the urgent radio broadcast, memories of his months as a rookie officer flooded back to the Brooklyn-born sergeant.

Guadioso recalled how he had first been assigned to Beat #141, the Lincoln Memorial, back in 1991 after graduating from the Federal Law Enforcement Training Center in Brunswick, Georgia. Upon completion of his eighteen weeks at the national academy, he returned to DC, where he spent several weeks on the beat with senior officers before being designated to the US Park Police's Central District, where he was assigned to his current post.

It was a duty that Guadioso and his fellow officers did

not take lightly. He and the others quickly realized that Beat #141 required its patrolmen to maintain a keen awareness of their surroundings at all times. Experience had taught them that a large number of suicides occur in National Parks, and that a fair share happened in their own jurisdiction at places such as the Vietnam Vet's Memorial. The commemorative monument had proven a favorite site for ex-servicemen, many bearing arms—either actual weapons or antique replicas.

Over the years, the sergeant had been summoned there to follow up on a number of "shots fired" calls. In some instances, his investigation revealed that the bullets were fired by accident, while others turned out to be a deliberate act of suicide.

Now, as he raced his motor scooter toward the pair of pay phones only a few hundred yards south of the Vietnam Memorial, his only thought was to find this guy with the gun before he could cause any harm—to himself or anybody else. The muffled sounds of tourists' voices in the distance distressed the officer as he sped his bike up close enough to the phones to observe that there was no one talking on either line. Suddenly, one of the phones began to ring, and he answered it to find Sergeant Farish of the Metro police on the other end of the line.

With the new information that Farish had given him, the sergeant searched the darkness, scouring the park for anyone fitting the dispatcher's description. Navigating the motorbike along the cement sidewalk that led to the Lincoln Memorial traffic circle, he made one last check and then headed south onto Constitution Avenue, rounded the 1900 block, and steered his scooter up onto the grassy area around Constitution Gardens. As he motored along, the single beam of his scooter's headlight illuminating tiny stretches of parkland, he was only vaguely aware of the pungent floral aroma that permeated the night air.

Guadioso hurried across the grassy expanse of parkland in the direction of The Wall. As he moved deliberately around the perimeter of the expansive granite monument, the sergeant instinctively fingered the cool metal handle of the German-made 9mm Glock that was holstered in his gun belt.

"We've located the suspect's vehicle," a familiar voice blared over Guadioso's radio. Slowing his scooter, the sergeant could hear his colleague, Sgt. Mike Russo, advising the operator that he had spotted a Mercury Mountaineer with Alabama tags #20CM895 on the twenty-first block of Constitution Avenue NW.

Guadioso paid close attention as Russo relayed how he had found the vehicle unoccupied and parked in a regular space on the south side of the lot. Directing his scooter toward the curb, he listened to Russo saying that he would station his cruiser near the vehicle and wait for the driver to return.

Checking his watch again, Sgt. Guadioso noted that it was now 12:50 a.m., thirty-four minutes since he was first alerted to a gunman on the loose. He parked his scooter on the east side of the Vietnam Vet's Memorial, and grabbing his flashlight, continued into the park on foot, firmly gripping the handle of his gun as he proceeded along the grass toward the impressive monument.

As he made his way around to the south side of The Wall, he observed movement in the shadows just up the hill from where he was standing. Shining his flashlight in that direction, he illuminated the figure of a man seated on the grass, just beyond the apex of the monument. He observed that the man was facing the memorial and that he had a shotgun positioned between his legs, the muzzle of the weapon pointing upward toward his mouth.

He could feel the adrenaline coursing through his veins as his eyes reflexively scanned the area, his attention immediately drawn to a small cluster of tourists milling about on the pathway on the south side of The Wall. Moving swiftly toward the group, he instinctively placed his body between them and the gunman.

"Let's get out of here!" he shouted, motioning them to run for cover. "There's a man with a gun!"

With an air of authority, he ushered the group to safety, and then radioed for backup. Before two words had escaped his mouth, he heard the deafening blast of gunfire echoing into the night. Pulling his weapon from its holster, he shouted into the radio strapped to his shoulder and rushed toward the suspect, gasping as he viewed the grisly sight— a dead man, his eyes wide open, his face grotesquely disfigured by the blast that had taken his life.

"I think we've got your guy," the US Park Police sergeant reported to Farish over the sergeant's cell phone.

Farish had been about to fax out the photograph of Jeremy Akers that he had just obtained when Guadioso's call came in. He and the other officers on Reservoir Road had been finishing up the processing of the crime scene, wrapping up an intense three-hour investigation.

Motioning to Detective Dwayne Partman, for whom this event marked his first time on a murder–suicide, Farish headed for his car. He knew that it was his responsibility to ID the suicide victim, and take over the homicide investigation from the Park Police.

When the officers arrived at the National Mall, they found crime scene tape encircling parts of the Memorial, and the prostate body of Jeremy Akers on the knoll behind it. He saw that the Mobile Crime Scene unit had already arrived, the same crew that had just finished up at Reservoir

Road. As Farish strode toward the body, the sergeant noticed that Detective Partman seemed hesitant. The thirty-nine-year-old officer had never been so close to a dead body. And neither had Sergeant Guadioso, who had remained on the scene to wait for the coroner's van to arrive.

Farish followed all the steps of police procedure, waiting as members of the crime scene unit snapped photographs and collected evidence. He watched as the men carefully wrapped the Mossberge 12-gauge shotgun with the 20" barrel and marked it as evidence, and as they collected the shotgun shell casing, as well as six shells they recovered from the gun's chamber.

Once the team had completed its job, Sergeant Farish rolled Jeremy's body over, and lifted up his blue fleece, zip-front pullover. Holstered in the small of his back was the .38 caliber pistol that he had used to kill his wife. In the front pocket of his blue jeans was the magazine clip and extra cartridges for the handgun.

As he viewed the body, Farish thought, "This is the only courageous thing this guy has done."

The sergeant helped the team load Jeremy's body into the black body bag and left it on the scene for the Medical Examiner.

When the coroner's van arrived, and the back doors were opened, Farish could see that there was another body on the truck. The sergeant knew immediately whose it was. With the help of Guadioso, the veteran homicide sergeant hoisted Jeremy's body onto the van, laying it carefully beside Nancy's.

EPILOGUE

THE POLICE CONTINUED TO SEARCH FOR JIM LEMKE, BUT their hunt did not yield any results until early the following morning. More than twelve hours after Nancy's murder, Sergeant Michael Farish received word that his officers had located the twenty-six-year-old truck driver. Jim's mother recalled her son telling her that when his lover failed to return home that night, he had gone out to look for her.

"What happened?" Jim quizzed the two uniformed policemen who approached him on the street outside of his apartment building. "Did her husband beat her up again?"

It was nearly ten a.m. when the men related to Jim that his girlfriend was murdered, shot to death by her estranged husband as she sat outside the family home in her red Jeep Wrangler.

Dissolving into uncontrollable sobs, Jim told the police he was too distraught to answer their questions. But the officers were irritated and admonished him to pull himself together for the sake of the children. They insisted that Jim assist them in sorting out the details of his girlfriend's life.

As police continued their investigation, Isabelle and Zeb remained at the home of their next-door neighbor. By early morning, Finny and his girlfriend had reached the District, having driven all night from the Outer Banks of North Carolina. When they arrived at his home on Reservoir Road, Finny noticed that a uniformed officer stood watch at the front door. Inside, police were conducting a thorough search of the premises, confiscating the camping equipment that Jeremy had used on his trip with Zeb and Isabelle the week before, and the note that he had scrawled on the back of an envelope.

Officers on the scene informed the Akerses' oldest son of his mother's death, and of his father's suicide. Although they understood his devastation, Finny was then tasked with the chore of telling his younger brother and sister what had happened to their parents, as friends and relatives from around the country descended on Washington, DC.

Nancy's mother, meanwhile, did not learn of her daughter's death until the following morning. After returning home with her family from church the following morning, Nancy's best friend, Emily, telephoned Susan Richards in Savannah, Georgia to offer her condolences. But it was immediately apparent to Emily that the elder woman had no idea what had happened. Upon hearing Emily's voice, Susan greeted her with a warm hello and the question, "To what do I owe the pleasure of this phone call?" The heartbreaking task of breaking the news to the victim's mother fell on Emily's shoulders. The memory of the scream with which Nancy's mother responded to the news still haunts Emily today.

Sensing that something was terribly wrong, Nancy's father, Roderick, got on the phone with Emily and tearfully explained that she was due to come for a visit in two weeks, a much-anticipated reconciliation that both parents could hardly wait for.

As the hours passed, and family members gathered, it was becoming increasingly clear that neither Nancy nor Jeremy had made any provisions for their minor children. There was no life insurance policy, no bank account, and no will. The only thing that police had turned up in their

search of the family home was the handwritten note left by
Jeremy. Minutes before his confrontation with Nancy, he
had stuffed the envelope with several thousand dollars in
cash, and then scribbled a monetary breakdown of the con-
tents and how he had intended it to be divided among his
three children.

In the weeks following the murder, friends of the couple
set up an education trust for the children, and asked that
donations be sent in care of their Washington, DC law firm.
Barbara Deane, owner of barbsbestbooks.com, an online
bookstore that specializes in romance novels, ran a contest
on her company's Website and raised $250 to donate to the
fund.

The absence of any last will and testament left the question of custody to be decided by family members. It was
clear that Susan and Roderick Richards and Gladys and
William Akers were too old to take on the responsibility of
raising two young children. Nancy's brothers, John and
Rod Richards, agreed that other family members might
make better choices as parents for Zeb and Isabelle.

That left Jeremy's two siblings, Carolyn and T, as the
only likely choices. Without hesitation, T and his wife, who
is also named Carolyn, moved to take custody of Zeb and
Isabelle. For Nancy and Jeremy, T would have been the
ideal choice. Friends of the couple agreed that both Nancy
and Jeremy loved and admired Jeremy's younger brother
and his wife, and without question would have wanted their
children in their custody. Not only was T intimately familiar with the youngsters from their countless visits to the
South, both he and his wife were successful, upstanding
members of their Florence, Alabama, community, and had
raised several children of their own.

Ironically, one of Jeremy's friends recalled how Jeremy
never really wanted his children growing up in the big city,

which he perceived to be dangerous and riddled with crime. On more than one occasion, he had voiced his desire to take the kids to Alabama and raise them in the country the way he had been raised.

When Susan and Roderick Richards arrived in town, Nancy's mother immediately took over the funeral arrangements being made for Nancy and Jeremy. Her husband was elderly and infirm, struggling with the debilitating effects of Alzheimer's disease.

In spite of his frail health, he had accompanied his wife to Washington, and to the morgue to identify the body of his beloved daughter. News of her death devastated him. But he retained his composure, and once at the morgue, he immediately noticed that police had copied her birth date from her driver's license incorrectly, and the coroner's office had catalogued her as three years younger than her actual age. The error was corrected on her death certificate, but was reported erroneously in the local newspapers.

Susan Richards' suggestion that the families hold a joint memorial service at the church where Zeb and Isabelle attended parochial school was met with raised eyebrows by friends and relatives of the deceased couple. But once Nancy's mother explained that she believed a single service would be best for the children, everybody rallied around her in support of the plan.

Many of Nancy's friends did not learn the disturbing news of her death until the following morning when they opened their Monday editions of *The Washington Post*. Right there on the front page was an article detailing the horrific events. "Romance Novelist Is Slain, Police Say Husband Killed Writer, Self," the headline read.

To many, the story was remarkable—and incomprehensible.

Alan Soschin, the lawyer handling Nancy's divorce case,

read the article in disbelief. As he skimmed the story, he ran to dial the Metropolitan Police Department for more details. Bewildered, he listened as the officer on the other end of the line explained what had happened.

He would later tell reporters, "I have a sense here that my client may have underestimated the emotional instability of her husband. . . . She was willing to try to work on the divorce. There was no reason for this to happen."

But as he sat behind the heavy wooden desk in his downtown office, recounting his conversations with Nancy Akers, he found himself completely shaken by her murder. In his twenty-six years practicing law, he had handled numerous cases in which he deemed it necessary to obtain a restraining order to protect a client whom he believed to be in danger. Yet, from all that Nancy had told him, and from the way that she acted during their meetings, he had no reason to believe that she was at risk. And he was certain that Jeremy's deadly attack had caught her completely off-guard.

News of Nancy's murder, and her husband's subsequent suicide, was carried in newspapers throughout the country, and around the world. Ray Walker learned of his friend's fate from someone in Sheffield who called to alert him after reading about the murder–suicide in their hometown gazette. Members of the Sheffield community were saddened and mournful upon learning of the death of their hometown hero.

As the days passed, published accounts alleged that Nancy had been abused by Jeremy, and the stories were bolstered with quotes pulled from emails that Nancy had written to several of her friends. The articles infuriated Finny, who maintained that his mother's electronic accusations were just not true. Other friends corroborated Finny's assertions.

Even close friends of the couple were puzzled, and many said that they had no knowledge of Jeremy physically abusing Nancy. Some speculated that her allegations of abuse were crafted to bolster her fight for custody of the children. One person who was very close to Nancy believed that she was "embellishing" on the truth to deflect attention from her abandonment of the children, and her extramarital affair with a man half her age.

In the weeks that followed Nancy's murder articles continued to appear in newspapers and on the World Wide Web, many painting Nancy as a battered woman, and drawing parallels between her murder and those of two other women in the romance community. One was a Silhouette Desires Series author named Pamela Macaluso who was killed in 1997 by her husband, Joseph. The Air Force missile specialist shot the author and their two teenage sons before taking his own life in the family's home at Vandenberg Air Force Base in Santa Barbara County. The other woman, Ann Wassall, was a college professor who taught courses in romance novels, who was murdered by her husband in 1996.

The stories alarmed authors of the romance community, who worried about the inference that romance writers were somehow targets of domestic abuse, and that the three deaths signaled a chilling trend.

At first, a mass was planned for the morning of June 8, and was to be primarily for members of the parochial school's community. But, after many of Nancy's and Jeremy's friends expressed interest in attending, the service was rescheduled for the evening of June 9, at Our Lady of Victory Catholic Church, and was open to anyone who wished to attend.

The day before the memorial service was to take place, thirty members of the WRW met at the home of Kathy

Seidel. Seated on comfortable chairs and couches in Kathy's airy living room, the authors remembered their friend, telling stories of their times with Nancy and mourning her death. They sipped tea and coffee from porcelain cups, and snacked on sandwiches and cookies that had been arranged and garnished in Nancy's elegant entertaining style.

The following evening, several of the authors attended the memorial service at Our Lady of Victory. To a standing-room-only crowd of mourners, Reverend William Foley delivered a eulogy that was strangely absent of any mention of the murder or suicide. He referred to the dead couple as "Our Brother Jeremy" and "Our Sister Nancy" and did not even allude to the fact that they were in the midst of divorce proceedings.

In the front row of the gracious stone chapel were Zeb, Isabelle, and Finny, who sat shoulder to shoulder with their grandparents, aunts, and uncles. The little girl kept her head down, her face hidden behind locks of her silky, blonde hair, as friends and relatives remembered her parents.

Nancy's brother, John Richards, read a letter to his sister, and talked about her many books. Jeremy's old Marine pal, Jonathan Blackmer, re-created snapshots of Vietnam by reading his friend's Silver Star Citation, hoping to share with the mourners a glimpse of the "real" Jeremy Akers.

Next, Nancy's divorce lawyer, Alan Soschin, infused a dose of reality into the service, explaining at what point the couple had been in the divorce process and talking about what was to follow. He directed many of his comments to the couple's children, alluding to letters that Nancy had written to him detailing how much she loved them.

Attired in an elegant black dress, her thick blonde hair catching the last rays of light that streamed in through the stained-glass windows, Jeremy's longtime friend, socialite

Patricia Duff, and another elegantly dressed woman took the podium.

Her voice cracked as she spoke of her final correspondence with Nancy. "Only twenty minutes before I heard the news, I was reading her last email. She was looking forward to spending two weeks with her children in Georgia."

Patricia had grown close to Nancy as both women tried to deal with the difficult men in their lives. Duff, everybody knew, was in the middle of a vicious custody battle with her estranged husband, Revlon billionaire Ron Perelman, at the same time that Nancy struggled to break her ties with her husband of twenty years.

About ten minutes into the service, one of Jeremy's friends noticed James Lemke quietly slip in through a rear door. "You're lucky to be alive," he whispered as Lemke stood with his back pressed up against the rear wall of the cathedral.

"I know," the young man answered in hushed tones. His expression revealed that he was clearly shaken by the comment.

Jeremy's friend turned his attention back toward the podium and listened as Kathy Seidel remembered her sister author. The attractive woman with the wavy brown hair explained that the value of romance is love, and hailed Nancy for showing her love through her social goodness and volunteerism.

After Kathy, several other people stood at the pulpit to remember Nancy and Jeremy before Finny's high school roommate stepped up to the microphone. His voice wavered as he spoke with admiration for his friend's dad, and then recalled a comment that Jeremy had made at one of his school football games: "When life hits you hard, hit back harder." The young man's pronouncement troubled several of Nancy's friends.

Finny's friend's recollection was followed by a few words from Nancy's father, Roderick Richards. The elderly man identified himself only as the children's grandfather. His slender frame draped in a conservative suit and tie, his hands clasping the podium, he told the roomful of friends and family that "every day is a blank slate." Addressing his grandchildren, he then said that it was important to "forgive, forget, and love each other."

At the end of the service, mourners were invited to join the family in a small reception area where cake and coffee were being served.

After the service, Zeb and Isabelle returned to their home on Reservoir Road with their Uncle T to pack their things for their journey to Alabama. Once inside the home, the children were unable to control their tears. As they struggled to gather their belongings, their bursts of emotion grew uncontrollable. Not wanting to cause them any further trauma, T and Carolyn opted to forgo the packing, leaving many of their possessions behind. Even the menagerie of animals and birds that Bill Ranger had watched and fed when the family went out-of-town was placed with a local animal adoption agency.

When they arrived at the Akerses' cozy home in Alabama, Zeb and Isabelle were given their own rooms. The children were immediately enrolled in counseling, and regularly joined their aunt and uncle at church services, which they attended every Wednesday and Sunday.

Finny joined his siblings in Alabama, renting a small flat just a few blocks away from his uncle's home. He enrolled at the University of Northern Alabama, the college his father had attended for his freshman and sophomore years, and then transferred to the University of Virginia, another of his father's alma maters, in the fall of 2000.

Bill Ranger continued to work to honor his friend's dying request that he be buried in Arlington National Cemetery. When he first began lobbying that Jeremy be laid to rest there, his request was met with resistance from the public. Angry letters were published in *The Washington Post* from readers who felt that Jeremy had dishonored himself when he killed his wife. Bill Ranger believed that his friend had been out of his mind when he shot Nancy that evening. He was convinced that Jeremy had not really thought out the consequences of his actions, and was certain that if he had, he never would have gone down the path that he did. Not only did he leave the children he so loved without a mother or father, but his crime of passion had also precluded him from being laid to rest in the burial place of his fellow war heroes.

For all of his efforts, Bill could not convince members of the United States Marine Corps to honor Jeremy Akers' dying wish. To them, Jeremy had broken the faith with the Marines by killing his wife.

Finally, Bill, with the help of a friend, Captain Bruce Dyer, USN (Ret) and his wife, LTC Connie Dyer, USAR, and Veteran's Affairs Chair, Florida State Council, arranged to have his friend's body shipped to Sheffield. There, eight members of the Vietnam Veterans of America, gave him a military-style burial that pleased Gladys and William Akers.

Being able to lay her father to rest helped Isabelle to come to terms with what had happened. But the little girl continued to fret over the fact that she had not been able to say goodbye to her mother in the same fashion. The ten-year-old continued to question why her grandmother, Susan Richards, was insisting on keeping Nancy's cremated ashes in an urn in her home, and not burying them in a proper service that she and her brothers could attend. To date, the situation remains unchanged. Susan continued to send cards and money to the children, and hosted a family get-together for the family at her home in Savannah, Georgia, two years after her daughter's death.

By all accounts, Zeb and Isabelle are said to be doing well, attending school and maintaining good grades. They even visited Washington, DC in the summer of 2000 to reconnect with friends there.

Three months after Sergeant Farish was called to the scene of the disturbing murder on Reservoir Road, he received a telephone call from a woman who expressed concern about Jim Lemke. Days after Nancy's murder, the young man told one reporter that "Nancy was a wonderful person." But, shortly after her memorial service, he dropped out of sight.

In the weeks that followed, Jim's mother revealed that her son was so distraught that he took weeks off from work, and went on a drinking binge that lasted for fourteen days. She also revealed that Jim had admitted to feeling responsible for Nancy's death, saying that he was disappointed at his inability to protect her. As the months passed, he continued to take her murder to heart, ultimately quitting his job and not answering his telephone.

When the call came in to the Metropolitan Police's Second District office, Sergeant Farish was working the midnight shift. Seated at his desk in his second-floor office he listened as a woman from Chicago, Illinois, who identified herself as a "concerned friend" of Jim's, explained that the twenty-six-year-old trucker had not been responding to her phone calls or emails. She said that she was worried that something might be wrong, and asked if police could go by to make sure that everything was all right.

It was the first time that Farish would meet the "poet king," who was all right, but continued to be distraught over Nancy's murder.

Shortly after Farish's visit, Jim Lemke left town, telling his mother that he was unable to remain in a city filled with the haunting memories of his love and his loss. Packing up Nancy's computer, which Mrs. Richards had promised to

Finny, he headed West. Despite his mother's pleas that he come home to Chicago, Jim remained on the road, phoning in from time to time to say that he was okay.

In the months that followed, the couple's friends struggled to make sense of the tragedy. Newspaper accounts pointed to Nancy's novels for clues.

But Nancy's friend Kathy Seidel said that readers would probably not find any easy answers. The bestselling author, who had gone on to write eleven romance novels under the name Kathleen Gilles Seidel explained: "There is, in many romance novels, something called the alpha male, who is distant and mysterious and a very conventional character type, and he is ultimately tamed by the heroine. I assume Nancy may have used that character type . . . I think if— and this is a big if—if she uses the alpha male character, tall, dark, handsome, mysterious man who looks like he is smoldering and has a quick temper, and you read the book and say, 'Ohmigod, this must be her husband,' you are wrong. This is seventy-five percent of what historical romances are like."

Kathy went on to say that she believed it would be impossible to find parallels between Nancy's real life and the characters she created.

"In romances, love solves the problem," Kathy explained. "It is never violence. Violence is never the answer. Love is always the answer, and so it's hard to look at whatever drove Jeremy Akers to do this."

Yet, as one skims Nancy's last novel, it is difficult to disregard passages such as these:

> "Ye're my wife and my place is with ye," Malcolm bent one knee on the bed, leaned forward, and with his arms on either side of Isobel, moved close enough to look her hard in the eye. "And ye best stop defying me . . ."